THE WELSH OF MERSEYSIDE

IN THE TWENTIETH CENTURY

VOLUME 2

D BEN REES

THE WELSH OF MERSEYSIDE

IN

THE TWENTIETH CENTURY

D BEN REES

*Illustrated with photographs from
a number of sources*

VOLUME 2

Modern Welsh Publications Ltd

THE WELSH OF MERSEYSIDE

IN

THE TWENTIETH CENTURY

First Published 2001

Published by Modern Welsh Publications Ltd,
Liverpool, England on behalf of the
Merseyside Welsh Millennium Committee.

Printed by the County Press, Bala, Gwynedd, Wales.

ISBN 0 901332 55 0

Preface

The history of the Welsh people on Merseyside deserves to be recorded. As J Saunders Lewis mentioned in a television interview with Aneirin Talfan Davies in 1960:

> "The idea that because I was born in Liverpool I was born an exile from Wales is completely false. I don't know what the statistics are, but I'm pretty sure that there were around about a hundred thousand Welsh-speaking people in Liverpool during the period of my boyhood. And I should say that at least half of those were monoglot Welsh speakers who could hardly manage a word of English."

Lewis was referring to the first decade of the twentieth century. Indeed I was given the task by the Merseyside Welsh Millennium Committee of preparing two volumes, one in Welsh and the other in English, on the Welsh of Merseyside in particular in the twentieth century. The reception to the two volumes, *Cymry Lerpwl a'r Cyffiniau* and The *Welsh of Merseyside*, published in 1997, has been very encouraging.

I decided on a different format for the current work. First of all I decided to provide one, or at the most two, entries for every year, supplementing them with photographs, in the main from the collections of John Thomas, Cambrian Gallery; E Emrys Jones of Colwyn Bay; and Dr John G Williams of Liverpool. These entries cover a wide range of topics so as to reflect the tremendous variety in the lives of the Liverpool Welsh, their leaders and communities, their interests and achievements.

I decided also, because of the rich tapestry, to include different biographies and accounts in the two volumes. In other words, the Welsh speakers, who naturally will buy the Welsh book, will be interested also in the English language volume, and vice versa. There are only half a dozen similar entries.

All this has meant additional work at a difficult time in my career. I am, however, very grateful for the support of the subscribers and those who generously donated towards this project.

The Merseyside Welsh Millennium Committee which I had the privilege to Chair did so much in the year 2000. We organized a brilliant re-union on Saturday 14th and Sunday 15th October at Bethel, Heathfield Road Presbyterian Church of Wales. Originally this book was to be launched at the Saturday night concert, but due to my numerous commitments and a period of hospitalization and convalescence it was not possible for it to be published then. Now I have completed the manuscript and am grateful to all those who helped in any way, and I look forward to its launch in the summer of 2001.

D Ben Rees
Liverpool
St Valentine's Day, 2001

Contents

Owen Elias Roberts; Pattern of a Welshwoman: Mrs Elisabeth Watcyn Thomas; A Labour MP lectures at Bootle on Ishmael Jones; Richard Huws returns to the University of Liverpool; The death of a distinguished Moderator of the Church; A Welshman as Head of the CID in Liverpool; A call by T I Ellis to the Liverpool Welsh to tour Wales; St David's Day celebrations in St Helens; A harp and a choir in the Preaching Festival at Huyton Quarry; The sudden passing of Kate Roberts's brother in Bootle.

1960-1969

No Trams to Lime Street; Liverpool Cymric in great voice; The obituary of a remarkable Liverpool Welsh missionary; The death of a retired company director; Fifty years with a city firm: Myfanwy Owen; First volume of the Wavertree Welsh poet; Arthur Rowland: a Garston bank manager, retires; Life and work of Enid Wyn Jones; A portrait of the Reverend Owen Prys Davies of Childwall; A portrait of the Reverend John David Williams Richards of Childwall.

1970-1979

Walton Prison Welsh Chaplaincy; Electing Presbyterian leaders; The closure of Whiston Welsh Chapel; An outstanding lecture by Owen Owen; A tribute to Dan Thomas; Fifty years as a Minister of Religion; Gosh it's Tosh; The skills of Kevin Ratcliffe of Everton FC; A novel on the Birkenhead Welsh; The retirement of the Reverend Robert Maurice Williams, minister at Waterloo and Southport.

1980-1989

Welsh boxer dies after title fight; Riots hit Toxteth; The magic of Ian Rush; Very Reverend Derrick Walters, fourth Dean of the Liverpool Anglican Cathedral; In praise of Goronwy Evan Thomas; Dewi-Prys Thomas, a talented architect; Neville Southall, Everton FC; Companion to Welsh Literature; A founder member of Family Link: Reverend Dafydd Hughes-Parry, of Woolton; Professor of Medicine at King Saud University; The life and work of Corwena Roberts of Whiston.

1990-1999

Welsh not Scouse; A Welsh childhood: Alice Thomas Ellis; A tribute to John Henry Roberts (Monallt); The Minister's son:
H Justin Evans; A tribute to Laura Myfanwy Jones; The portrait of a surgeon: Wil Lloyd Jones; Roy Watterson of Liverpool and Australia; A biography of Dr R Arthur Hughes; The life and work of the Reverend John Meirion Lloyd; A welcome to Llanelli Male Voice Choir; Biography: Dr E Wyn Jones.

Appendix A: A thanksgiving for the life and work of Gwen Vaughan Jones.

Appendix B: List of donations.

Appendix C: List of subscribers.

A new Welsh chapel at Edge Lane

■ *The house of the generous Holyrood Edge Lane family in Calderstones.*

At the beginning of 1899, the leaders and members of Holt Road Welsh Calvinistic Methodist Chapel bought a piece of land at Edge Lane, opposite Botanic Road and Wavertree Park, on which today stands an Indian temple. Haugh & Pilling built the chapel and the schoolrooms in accordance with the designs of Richard Owen & Son. It was opened on Wednesday, 3 October 1900 with a service of preaching, and this was the pattern on the Thursday, Friday, Saturday and Sunday with a mixture of local as well as popular national preachers of the calibre of Dr Cynddylan Jones of Cardiff, and Reverend Dr D Lloyd Jones of Llandinam.

The new building could cater for seven hundred, though the membership was only three hundred and nineteen. Its size reflected the optimism of the belief that organized religious observance among the Welsh was set to double in the next few decades. The cost came to £7,146 and the sum of £1,050 was received from the sale of premises in Holt Road, which were bought by the United Methodist denomination. The members contributed over £2,600 but a debt of over £3,000 still remained. It was finally cleared a decade later, in 1910.

Elfed's biography of Dr Evan Herbert Evans

Welshmen of all persuasions were delighted at the reception given by the English press to the biography, Life of Dr Herbert Evans, published in 1901, in London by Hodder & Stoughton. *"No book,"* declared the eminent literary critic Dr Robertson Nicoll, *"will do more to interpret Welsh religious life to the English and Scotch peoples."* The works fall into four parts: Preparatory Years (1836-1862); First period of Ministry (1865-1879); Darkened Noon (1880-1884) and Closing Years (1885-1896).

Dr Herbert Evans had close connections with Liverpool. He arrived there in 1854, became associated with Tabernacle Independent Chapel and was inspired by its minister, Reverend Dr John Thomas. His only daughter Lizzie became the wife of the Reverend O L Roberts, another outstanding minister attached to the Independent Chapels in Liverpool.

His biographer, Reverend Elvet Lewis, now known simply as Elvet or in Welsh, Elfed, was a very fine minister of the same denomination and laboured at King's Cross Chapel, London for forty years. Dr Robertson Nicoll said of him:

"Mr. Elvet Lewis himself is a man of rare gifts. He is a poet, a mystic, a theologian, and a stylist." This is a tribute worth repeating, and he was very much a favourite visiting preacher and lecturer in the Merseyside Welsh communities for sixty years, since he first came to Buckley, Flintshire in 1880.

■ *Reverend Dr John Thomas*

Herbert Evans was an outstanding Welsh preacher. English audiences crowded into Exeter Hall and the Metropolitan Tabernacle in London to hear him, and having heard him, they rapturously testified that they had heard no man speak with such authority. But he was even more

■ *Reverend O.L. Roberts*

eloquent in his mother tongue. For as Elvet showed in his biography, Herbert was first and last a Welsh language preacher. So were Reverend Dr John Williams of Princes Road, Liverpool and Hugh Jones of Douglas Road Welsh Chapel, two other preachers of early 20th Century Merseyside.

The life of William Rathbone

William Rathbone VI was born in 1819. He became much involved with Wales in November 1880, on being elected Liberal Member of Parliament for Caernarfonshire; when, in 1885, the constituency was divided, he continued to represent its northern division until 1895, retiring because he disagreed with the political nationalism of the younger figures in the party, such as Tom Ellis and David Lloyd George. He did a great deal for the University College of North Wales at Bangor and the University of Liverpool, and supported the National Eisteddfod of Wales when it came to his native city in 1900. He contributed generously to, and collected money from among the merchant princes of Liverpool for the centres of higher education. As a Unitarian he highly regarded the heritage of the denomination in the Teify Valley in Cardiganshire and knew those Welshmen who served Unitarianiam in Liverpool, like George Eyre Evans (1857-1939), author of *History of Renshaw Street Chapel, Liverpool*, published in 1887, and *Record of the Provincial Assembly of Lancashire* and Cheshire, published in 1896. William Rathbone died in Liverpool on 6 March 1902.

Further reading

William Rathbone: *Social Duties*, London, Macmillan & Co, 1867; William Rathbone, *History of District Nursing*, London, Macmillan & Co, 1890 and his biography written by his daughter, see Eleanor F. Rathbone, *William Rathbone: A Memoir*, London, Macmillan & Co, 1905.

E. Emrys Jones

■ *University College of North Wales, Bangor*

Young Wales in Bootle

Young Wales (Cymru Fydd) was a movement established by the London Welsh in 1886 along the lines of Young Ireland. One of the best known of the early members of the movement, namely the historian Sir John Edward Lloyd, came from the Liverpool Welsh Community, and the whole story has been narrated in Welsh by the Criccieth solicitor, William George (brother of David Lloyd George) in **Cymru Fydd: Hanes y Mudiad Cenedlaethol Cyntaf** published in 1945, in Liverpool by Brython Press.

In 1903 a branch of Cymru Fydd was opened in Bootle with Job Jones of Cromwell House, as President, and William George (father of the Reverend A J George, a scholarly Welsh Baptist, minister for most of his life at Tyddynshôn, near Four Crosses, in Caernarfonshire). William George of 55 Cambridge Road, Bootle served as Secretary for the rest of the decade, keeping alive the idealism of the Young Wales movement among his fellow Welsh compatriots. They had plans to build a new centre and in the 1906 general election over one hundred Welsh men and women who belonged to Young Wales campaigned for the Liberal candidate, Dr A D Thomas.

■ *Miller's Bridge scene in yesteryear and the home of the first Welsh Chapel in Bootle*

The 'Love-Song' of the 1904-1906 Revival

■ *Reverend Griffith Ellis, minister of Stanley Road, Bootle who took a leading role in extending the invitation to the revivalist Evan Roberts to Merseyside*

■ *Mrs Griffith Ellis, a product of the Liverpool Welsh community*

Annie Davies of Maesteg had tears in her eyes and grace in her heart as she sang the mighty 'love-song' of the 1904-1906 Welsh Religious Revival which took place all over Wales and in Liverpool. The spiritual love-song of the Welsh nation was the hymn written by the 19th Century Liverpool Welsh poet and preacher, Dr William Rees (Gwilym Hiraethog). Reverend Elvet (Elfed) Lewis of London translated the hymn into English:

Wondrous Love, Unbounded Mercy!
Vast as oceans in their flood;
Jesus, Prince of Life, is dying!
Life for us in His blood!
Oh! What heart can e'er forget Him,
Who can cease His praise to sing –
Wondrous Love! For ever cherished
While the Heavens with music ring.

Rent on Calvary asunder
Were the fountains of the deep;
Nor within their ancient channels
Could the streams of mercy keep:
See the overflowing torrents
Of redeeming Love and Grace
Peace Divine and perfect Justice;
Now a guilty world embrace.

The original hymn, starting *"Dyma gariad fel y moroedd"*, is still sung in the Welsh chapels of Merseyside in the year 2001.

■ *Gwilym Hiraethog*

Appreciation of Dr Isaac Roberts, FRS, FRAS

Dr Isaac Roberts was an acknowledged astronomer; though his life and work belongs to the 19th Century, he did survive into the twentieth, and his remains were laid to rest at Flaybrick Hill Cemetery, Birkenhead, where a memorial was placed by his widow Dorothea Roberts (née Klumpke) who was herself a well-known astronomer.

Born in a small hamlet called Groes ('Cross') outside Denbigh on the edge of the Hiraethog Moors, on 27 January 1829, Isaac Roberts sailed as a child to the USA with his parents, but they returned to Liverpool. There he was apprenticed to a company of building contractors, Messrs Johnson. He became a prominent figure in the company and extremely affluent. However he spent his leisure time as an astronomer. He built observatories at Rock Ferry and Maghull on Merseyside and later at Crowborough, Sussex, where he died suddenly on 17 July 1904. Taking photographs of the stars was his main delight, and his Photographs of Stars, Star-Clusters and Nebulae was published in two volumes. He was a fervent Welshman and his will left legacies for the University of Wales (Bangor and Cardiff University Colleges) and the University of Liverpool.

He was one of the pioneers of astronomy within the Welsh nation and a worthy obituary appeared in Welsh in the magazine *Genhinen* (1904). It was compiled by his fellow astronomer and great friend from the Liverpool Welsh community, Eleazar Roberts (1825-1912).

Eleazar Roberts translated into Welsh the two volumes of the work of Dr Dick of *The Solar System* and frequently lectured on astronomy in various parts of Wales. He and Dr Isaac Roberts met each other frequently and exchanged notes on the world of astronomy. Isaac Roberts made his money as a builder in Liverpool. He retired in 1888 so that he could devote all his energies to astronomy. An honorary Doctor of Science from Trinity College, Dublin was given to him in 1892, and in 1895 he was awarded the R.A.S. gold medal.

Grief of a Welsh family in Normanby Street

Within two months of each other, a mother and daughter died. They had lived at 5 Normanby Street, Liverpool. On Sunday morning, 26 August 1905, Miss Winnie Williams died at the Royal Southern Hospital. She was the third daughter of the late David Williams of Daisy Street, Anfield, a native of Pwllheli, and his wife, Mrs Annie Williams. The father died as a result of an accident as a carpenter in 1890 and left his widow, a son and six daughters to mourn him.

The eldest daughter, Annie Williams, dedicated her talents to missionary work on the Khasia Hills, India and died of typhoid after the 1897 earthquake. Three of the daughters were teachers and Winnie Williams taught also in the Sunday Schools in Arnot Street, Garmoyle Road and in the Welsh Free Church at Upper Canning Street. The funeral was held on August 30th, at Smithdown Road Cemetery with the Rev W O Jones and Noah Bevan officiating.

On Monday night, October 19th, Annie, the mother, died at the age of fifty-six. Born at Bryneglwys, near Corwen, her parents moved to Liverpool in 1852 when she was only three years of age. She was a product of Bedford Street and Princes Road Welsh Calvinistic Methodist Chapels and, after her marriage, she moved to Anfield Road Calvinistic Methodist Chapel. She and her family became involved with the new movement, the Welsh Free Church, a literal translation of *Eglwys Rydd y Cymry* and they were associated with the chapels in Merton Road, Bootle, Garmoyle Road, Wavertree and then Upper Canning Street. A wise woman, she was full of common sense, strong character and godliness tinged with practical concerns. It was said of her:

> *"Her heart was tender and her hand generous – she loved to give from her own scarce resources."*

The funeral took place in Smithdown Road Cemetery, Monday afternoon, October 22nd , and on the following Sunday evening a sermon in memory of Annie Williams was preached at Upper Canning Street Chapel by the movement's founder, Rev W O Jones.

The Liverpool Welsh entrepreneur crosses the Atlantic

◀ *Owen Owen*

On 27 March 1906, Owen Owen, a Liverpool-Welsh draper, set sail from his adopted city to North America. His nephew Bob Davies accompanied him. Owen Owen had considerable holdings in sixteen different railroad companies in the United States of America. His turnover of shares in the Erie Railroad, the Pennsylvania Railroad and the Illinois Central Railroad was in excess of a quarter of a million pounds in 1901.

He was excited to be travelling on the liner *"Carmania"*, a large boat (650 feet in length) launched on Clydeside in 1905. He wrote to his wife on March 30th in the middle of the Atlantic of that vessel and her captain:

> *"She is splendid, it has been fine but enough roughness about to have closed me down in any ordinary boat, here I am all the time enjoying the breeze immensely. Both Captain Pritchard, a Welshman from Caernarvon though living in Liverpool, and his six officers appear to me capable men..."*

Owen and his nephew travelled all over North America. It was an eye opener to him. In the end, he realised that most of the ideas implemented in New York and elsewhere, were basically those which he had considered in Liverpool and London, but not implemented.

The pair arrived back in the middle of May, completely exhausted after the journey of a lifetime.

■ *A family tradition: Mrs Owen presents gold watches to long serving members of the staff*

Unsurpassed children's choir of Everton Village

One cannot think of a more successful children's choir than the Welsh Children's Choir of Everton Village, as it was known. It was established in 1899 and associated with the Band of Hope which was in turn associated with the Welsh Baptist Chapel of Everton Village. The founder was R T Edwards, a young man of twenty-one who became its conductor. He was a member of the chapel and his aim was to raise the standard of choral music among children. By 1907 he had taken over Oak Hall in Oakfield Road, Anfield (which at one time was the centre for the Young Wales Movement of Anfield) and the office of the Liverpool Musical Festival for Children, which began through the efforts of this choir and musicians from the Liverpool-Welsh community.

This choir was unsurpassed and won the chief prize for children's choirs at the National Eisteddfod of Wales in Rhyl (1904), Caernarfon (1906) and Swansea (1907). It was decided after this to concentrate on concerts rather than competing at the Merseyside eisteddfoddu and similar gatherings in Wales.

■ *Advertising the spiritual activities of Everton Village Chapel*

Reverend John Owen at Anfield Road

Born in 1855 at Aberllefenni, near the quarrying village of Corris in Merionethshire, John Owen had abundant educational opportunities at Bala, the University of Wales at Aberystwyth and at the University of Oxford. He suffered a great deal from illness and was unable to complete his studies at Oxford. Owen returned home and was ordained by the Welsh Calvinistic Methodists to take charge of the Chapel of Aberllefenni before moving from there to Aberdovey, then on to Bethesda Chapel, Mold, before receiving a call to Anfield Road Chapel, Liverpool, in 1908, as a successor to the Reverend Owen Owens. The number of members at Anfield Road at that time, was six hundred and thirty-four. He ministered there for ten years and in 1912 he was elected Moderator of the North Wales Association.

Owen had a great interest in missionary work. A large mission hall was built in South Street and opened in 1914 superseding the mission rooms in William Moult Street and Daisy Street. There he was assisted by a succession of missionaries, Reverend Ifor Hael Jones (1913-15), Reverend Owen Hughes (1916-17) and Sister Kate Evans. Health problems led to his resignation in 1918. They moved to Southport and then, in November 1921, to West Kirby where he was invited to be the minister of the Welsh Chapel for a period of five years. He stayed for nearly six years before retiring to Cressington, a pleasant suburb of South Liverpool, and he became a member of the Welsh Chapel in Garston.

His wife was a very capable Sunday School teacher, and I have known a number who were in her Sunday School class at Garston.

John Owen had a passion for writing biographies. He wrote three, one of a preacher at Mold, Reverend Robert Owen, Tŷ Draw (father of the Reverend William Owen, first minister of Webster Road Calvinistic Methodist Chapel in Liverpool) on of the doyen of Welsh novelists, Daniel Owen and finally a biography of the Reverend Griffith Ellis of Bootle. This was a very worthwhile endeavour.

In 1914, during his stay at West Kirby, he became Moderator of the General Assembly of the Presbyterian Church of Wales. He died on 28 September 1931 and his grave can be seen at Anfield Cemetery, Liverpool.

Augustus John paints the retiring Lord Mayor

The Bohemian Welsh artist, Augustus John, loved Liverpool and yet was to land himself in great trouble in 1909 when he painted the retiring Lord Mayor. This was a presentation portrait to H Chaloner Dowdall. The finished item, with Dowdall as a heavily dramatised civic Don Quixote and a rubicund footman called Smith as his Sancho Panza, took little account of civic pride and upset so many of its citizens, in particular the somewhat sensitive press, the Liverpool Post called it *"...either an extremely bad practical joke, or else the grossest exhibition of bad and unartistic taste we have seen on the walls of the gallery..."*

Augustus John was deeply upset at the criticism. He found it *"stupid, disgusting and unnecessary"*. Dowdall defended the Welsh artist, but within ten years had sold the picture to a private buyer in Sussex who offered him £1,400 for it, that is fourteen times John's original fee. Dowdall's wife persuaded him to accept the offer of £1,400 rather than the Tate Gallery's offer of £300. It never found a home in Liverpool and in 1938 it went off to the National Gallery of Victoria at Melbourne, Australia – the year the Walker Art Gallery bought the *"Two Jamaican Girls"*, its first example of Augustus John's work.

In 1950 the Walker Gallery borrowed the picture from Melbourne, and H C Dowdall, in his nineties, revealed much about the circumstances of the painting and of his friendship with Augustus John.

■ *A portrait of John Sampson of the University of Liverpool and author of* **The Dialect of the Gypsies of Wales** *by Augustus John*

The tragedy of "Kate Thomas"

The sailing ship *"Kate Thomas"* was very much a product of Liverpool-Welsh effort. It was built by the Doxford Company in Sunderland to the specifications of the Port Dinorwic designer W E Jones, and under the inspiration of the Liverpool-Welsh ship owner William Thomas. The cost of building it came to £16,477-10s-0d, and Thomas offered shares of £100 each. Seventy-nine investors responded to the offer. Some were ministers like Reverend Owen Owens of 37 Anfield Road and Reverend Evan Jones of Caernarfon (one share each) whilst others were wealthy capitalists, like the builder David Hughes, of JP Fenwick Court, Liverpool and Owen Owens, of 16 Well Lane, Tranmere. William Thomas himself bought the largest block of shares, eighteen of them.

Welsh sailors became the captains of *"Kate Thomas"*, named after William Thomas's first wife – men of the calibre of Captain Charlie Hughes, of Holyhead, Captain Thomas Williams of Treborth, Captain Seth Hughes of Bangor and Captain Henry Thomas, a devout Baptist Deacon of Caernarfon.

The end came to *"Kate Thomas"* in 1910, after twenty years of sailing the oceans. At four o'clock on a foggy morning in April that year, as the boat returned from Antwerp to Port Talbot and Liverpool, it collided with the steamship *"India"* and within eight minutes *"Kate Thomas"*, the captain and his wife and sixteen members of the crew had disappeared forever. The only crew member to survive was a young apprentice by the name of John Nelson. The Captain was John Williams, thirty-two years of age, the son of a farmer on the outskirts of Caernarfon, who had married Miss Hughes of Marian-glas, Anglesey. They had plans to build a house in the village of Moelfre in Anglesey. The first mate was William Roberts, a native of Abersoch and his wife was also a Hughes before marriage, the daughter of Mr and Mrs Owen Hughes of Afonwen near Pwllheli. They lived at 25 Ala Road, Pwllheli.

The loss of the crew and the sinking were devastating blows for the villages in Anglesey and Caernarfonshire and caused grief in Liverpool Welsh circles and among the kith and kin of William Thomas. The shareholders all received compensation through the insurance cover, but nothing could compensate for the human tragedy.

The return of Thomas Isfryn Hughes to Liverpool

Thomas Isfryn Jones was a well-known Welsh Wesleyan Methodist Minister in Liverpool. Born on 16 October 1865 in Clocaenog, Denbighshire, he was ordained to the Methodist Church in 1887. He moved to Liverpool in 1902 to care for the Mynydd Seion Circuit and he was in the city during the outpourings of the Welsh Religious Revival (1904-1905) associated with Evan Roberts. He came back for a second period in 1911 and in 1914 moved to care for another circuit in Liverpool namely the Oakfield Circuit. During this period he became President of the Welsh Wesleyan Conference in 1918.

■ *From left Nanw Williams, Gwen Herbert and Lilian Smith pictured in their handmade traditional Welsh costumes in the grounds of Bron y Garth, Porthmadog.*

His wife Catherine (née Jenkins) hailed from Aberdovey. They left Liverpool in 1919 for Porthmadog and retired in 1931, moving to Trearddur Bay in Anglesey where Thomas died on 27 December 1942. He was a conscientious author and a keen theological student, as can be seen from his articles in the **Geiriadur Beiblaidd** (the Biblical Dictionary) and in his commentary on the Epistle to the Phillipians and Philemon. He had shown enormous energy during his ministries in Liverpool from 1902-1905 and 1911-1919.

E. Emrys Jones

■ *Colwyn River at Beddgelert and the signpost for Porthmadog where T Isfryn Hughes ministered after leaving Liverpool.*

The loss of a Temperance Leader

■ *Reverend John Cadvan Davies ('Cadvan' 1846-1923) a Liverpool Wesleyan Methodist minister, whom Gwilym Dafydd adored.*

In religion he was a Wesleyan Methodist, educated at the Methodist School in Leeds Street. As a child he attended the Methodist chapel of Burrough's Gardens at the time of the Reverend Thomas Aubrey and J B Chambers. He moved with that church to Boundary Street, and later to Spellow Lane where he served as an elder for forty-three years.

The funeral took place on Monday, November 19th at Spellow Lane Chapel, with the Reverend J Felix officiating. Sympathy was expressed to his wife, the daughter of David Griffiths who had been an Archdruid and known as Clwydfardd. The tribute of the Reverend J O Williams, the influential Liverpool Welsh minister known as Pedrog, was profound as well as simple:

On 15 November 1912 at his home, 77 Everton Terrace, William Davies, known by his bardic name of Gwilym Dafydd, died at the age of eighty-two. A native of Towyn, Merionethshire, he came to Liverpool when he was four years of age. Recognised as a staunch Temperance leader throughout much of his long life, he served from 1878 until 1912 as the Secretary of the Temperance Union.

> *"Yes, a very good man was William Davies, in all his ways."*

The departure of the Reverend John Roberts to Cardiff

John Roberts was the Minister of the Welsh Calvinistic Methodist Chapel of David Street in the Dingle from 1906 until 1913. He was born on 16 October 1890 in Porthmadog, the son of a well-known poet-preacher, Reverend John Jones Roberts, known by his poetic name of Iolo Caernarfon, and his wife Ann. He was educated locally, then at Bala Grammar School, and Jesus College Oxford where he graduated in the Classics and in Theology. His first pastorate was in Aberdovey and he moved from there to Liverpool to care for David Street Chapel. Roberts spent seven years in Liverpool before moving to Cardiff to take charge of Pembroke Terrace Chapel until 1938, when he accepted the invitation to take charge of the administration of the Presbyterian Church of Wales. Reverend John Roberts is generally regarded as an important and influential figure in its history.

He possessed a gift as an historian, and his two volumes on the Presbyterian Church of Wales (the Welsh version appeared in 1931 and the English in 1934) are outstanding contributions to the understanding of the ethos and philosophy of the Welsh Methodist Movement.

In 1903 Reverend John Roberts married Annie Jones Lewis of Porthmadog, and four sons and two daughters were born to them. He died on 29 July 1959.

■ *Professor RT Jenkins (1881-1969), the Welsh historian and a bosom friend of John Roberts. Robert Thomas Jenkins was born in Liverpool on the 3rd August 1881. He was three years old when his parents moved to Bangor.*

August and after

At eleven o'clock at night on August 4th, Great Britain declared war on Germany. **_The Liverpool Daily Post and Mercury_** had published an announcement the previous day informing all Cammell Laird's workers that the traditional August week's holiday had been cancelled owing to urgent work and that they should report to the shipyard in Birkenhead the following morning. Part of the urgent work would be to build over thirty warships for the Royal Navy.

Many of the Cammell Laird workers were Welsh. They were back home on holiday and the assassination of an Archduke, in a far-off place called Sarajevo, meant very little to Birkenhead Welshmen on holiday in Llanuwchllyn or Llansantffraid yn Mechain. When, however, they returned to Birkenhead, the full impact was soon felt. Many of their friends from the Welsh chapels had joined the forces, and it quietly dawned on many of them that they had very little choice

■ *A brochure produced by Stanley Road Welsh Chapel, Bootle of all the young soldiers who fought in the First World War*

but to respond to the pressure to do likewise. On August 7th, Field Marshall Earl Kitchener of Khartoum made his first appeal for one hundred thousand men to serve the army for the duration of the conflict. His famous pointing finger poster, drawn by Alfred Leete, was to follow later.

By August 23rd, a new battalion had been formed in Liverpool, based at Seaforth Barracks, and Lord Kitchener was informed that it was ready for duty. The 11th Battalion was, by my reckoning, the first service battalion to be raised in Britain, and it would serve throughout the war as a pioneer unit. There were twenty-seven Liverpool Welshmen in its ranks.

The life of Hugh Jones *(Mulgrave Street)*

Born in Holyhead in 1852, Hugh Jones came to Merseyside with his father, Richard Jones, at a very early age. Richard was involved in the building industry but it was Hugh who enlarged the business and began, in partnership with another Angleseyman, John Lewis of Cemaes, to build houses in the Toxteth area. They were responsible for building houses in Mulgrave Street and Kimberley Street on Parliament Fields. His next venture was to build in Alwyn Street and Chetwynd Street, off Aigburth Road in St. Michael's in the Hamlet area, in partnership with his brothers John, William and Edward, under the name of Jones Brothers.

With his brother Edward Jones (1854-1939), who had been born in Llanfechell, he built in Spekeland, Luxor, Memphis and Serdar Streets, all in the Edge Hill area. Then he took on his own son, Edward R Jones, into partnership on a very important project. Their task was to replace houses which had been condemned and demolished by the Liverpool Corporation. They did extensive work

in Aigburth on the Woodlands Estate and on the Biarley, Valley Field and Mossdale Estates.

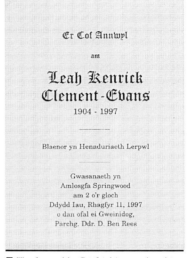

Er Cof Annwyl

am

Leah Kenrick Clement-Evans

1904 - 1997

Blaenor yn Henaduriaeth Lerpwl

Gwasanaeth yn
Amlosgfa Springwood
am 2 o'r gloch
Ddydd Iau, Rhagfyr 11, 1997
o dan ofal ei Gweinidog,
Parchg. Ddr. D. Ben Rees

■ *The funeral leaflet for his grandaughter, Leah Kenrick Clement-Evans in 1997*

A versatile individual, Hugh Jones served as a Commissioner of Income Tax and Land Tax, as well as serving for years on the Toxteth Board of Guardians and as a Justice of the Peace in Liverpool. A founder of the Young Wales Society in Upper Parliament Street, he attended regularly and donated generously to the Princes Road Calvinistic Methodist Chapel. He was mourned by many at his death in November 1915.

Bardcraft in his blood

Rolant Wyn Edwards, a native of Trawsfynydd, Merionethshire, was deeply involved in Welsh life in the first three decades of the 20th Century. He won many bardic trophies as a Welsh poet including an Eisteddfod in his home village of Trawsfynydd and served with distinction as an elder at Parkfield Welsh Presbyterian Chapel, Birkenhead. He served as a caretaker in South John Street and later at the City Buildings, Old Hall Street, Liverpool.

But poetry ran deep in Rolant's blood. His nephew, the shepherd poet, Ellis Evans, known as Hedd Wyn (also of Trawsfynydd), won the chair for an ode to *"The Hero"* at the National Eisteddfod of Wales, held at Birkenhead Park in 1917. That achievement will live forever in the memories of Merseyside Eisteddfodwyr, if only for the fact that tragedy was conjoined with triumph during the chairing of the bard. News was received a few days before the festival that the winner

■ *The statue of Hedd Wyn at Trawsfynydd.*

of the Eisteddfod Chair had been killed in action in France. Profound sorrow marked the ceremony and the empty chair, draped in the colour of mourning, became known as *"Cadair Ddu Birkenhead"* (the Black Chair of Birkenhead).

■ *A typical street in Trawsfynydd, the birthplace of Rolant Wyn*

The life of a cultured Liverpool Welsh builder

William Owen Elias of Mere House, Everton, was the son of Mr and Mrs Owen Elias. The father, Owen Elias (1806-1880), was known as King of Everton and became a wealthy and generous Welsh builder. William was born in Liverpool in 1850 and, after his initial education, entered his father's business, later becoming a partner, and was responsible for a large number of houses built in Anfield and Walton.

Aside from his business affairs, William maintained a passionate interest in the preservation of the Welsh language and literature. He acquired a well-stocked library of Welsh books and later in life bequeathed them to the University College of Wales at Aberystwyth, where he was a long-standing member of the Court of Governors.

In 1870 he married Martha Williams and they had three sons and three daughters. Martha was the daughter of William Williams, one of the early Welsh councillors serving on Liverpool's Town Council. It became known as the City Council in 1880.

William Owen Elias followed his father in taking great interest in Welsh Calvinistic Methodism, and became an asset to the Welsh Chapel in West Kirby. He died in West Kirby in 1917. Two of his sons became very interested in cultural and literary matters. Charles F Elias became a member of the Liverpool City Council while Frank Elias wrote several books, including **Beautiful Ships** and **The Blitz Hero.**

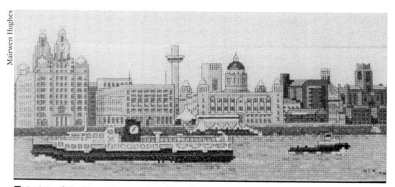

Mairwen Hughes

■ *A view of the River Mersey enjoyed by Charles and Frank Elias and worked in cross stitch by Maxi Roberts of Rhosymeirch, near Llangefni and late of Liverpool.*

An enthusiastic Eisteddfodwr

Among the enthusiastic, cultured intellectuals of the Merseyside Welsh Community, one has to give pride of place to Reverend David Adams who arrived in 1895 as Minister of Liverpool's Grove Street Welsh Independent Chapel. He died on 5 July 1923 and was buried in his native village of Talybont, near Aberystwyth on July 10th.

David Adams, known in bardic circles as Hawen, won the crown at the National Eisteddfod of Wales, held at Swansea in 1891, and was naturally very involved when the National Eisteddfod came to Liverpool in 1900 and to Birkenhead in 1917. He was one of the enthusiasts who supported the formation of an Eisteddfod catering for children, to be held annually in Birkenhead, and to be known as "Eisteddfod y G'lomen Wen", the Eisteddfod of the White Dove.

David Adams travelled on the ferry in all weathers from Liverpool to Birkenhead and as late as 1918, at the age of seventy-three, he attended the executive meetings of "Eisteddfod y G'lomen Wen". He was determined

■ *Reverend David Adams*

that the children and youth of the Welsh community should enjoy the same background as he had cherished throughout his life. He wrote poetry to inspire them to practise the language of the Welsh people.

The life of John Francis of Birkenhead

A native of Rhosybol in Anglesey, John Francis was fortunate in being apprenticed to William Hughes of Llawenllwyfo, Dulas, and through this initial training came, in 1881, at the age of eighteen, to Liverpool to work for Hugh Lewis, a builder and a native of Llaneilian near Amlwch.

By 1884 John Francis was a fully-fledged builder, concentrating his efforts on Birkenhead. He was responsible for the houses that were built in Cleveland, Livingstone and Vittoria Streets, Grange Road West, Park Road South and Francis Avenue, all in the town of Birkenhead. Then he built Seymour Street in High Tranmere, and Buchanan Road and Lincoln Drive in Wallasey.

An ardent Liberal in politics, John Francis took an active part in all the elections, and was very supportive of W H Lever (later Lord Leverhulme). He devoted a great deal of time with his pony and trap to canvassing on behalf of Lever (1861-1925), who built a model village (nine hundred houses for a population of three thousand workers) at the Lever Brothers' Soap Factory on the Wirral. Port Sunlight is a village created by the philanthropic industrialist and great friend of John Francis.

The Birkenhead Welsh builder died at his residence, 45 Park Road South, in 1919.

■ *Edward Evans Junior, JP of Spital Old Hall, Spital and for sixteen years Chairman of Wirral Liberal Association and a colleague of John Francis.*

Achievements of Robert John Rowlands *(Meuryn)*

Robert John Rowlands was a journalist, poet and zealous supporter of Welsh life and culture in Liverpool. Born at Abergwyngregyn near Bangor on 22 May 1890, he received his education at Aber Board School when the Welsh Not was in operation. He came to Liverpool as a young lad to work in the office of the Welsh printer and publisher, Isaac Foulkes, and except for a short period at Porthmadog, he spent over twenty-five years in Liverpool. He became correspondent to the Welsh weekly **Y Darian** and to the **Herald Gymraeg,** indeed he became the overseer of the Liverpool edition of the Caernarfon based Herald.

Rowlands was very prominent in the Welsh life of Liverpool, and one of the founders of the Union of the Red Dragon and an enthusiastic helper with regard to its successful, annual Eisteddfod. He would write poetry for the Welsh Press, and he became well-known by the early decades of the 20th Century for his verse. His only volume of poetry, called **Swynion Serch,** appeared in 1906. He was resident in Liverpool when he won the Chair at the Eisteddfod in Bethesda in

NLW Aberystwyth

■ *RJ Rowlands:'Meuryn'*

1919, under the adjudication of R Williams Parry, and then the Chair at the National Eisteddfod of Wales in 1920 for his awdl *"Min-y-Môr".* He moved in November of that year to Caernarfon, and I remember very well the thrill of reading two of his numerous Welsh children's books as they emerged from the press, the first being **Chwedlau'r Meini** in 1946, and then two years later **Dirgelwch Plas y Coed** (a detective novel). He was editor of the Herald Gymraeg and other papers in Caernarfon, after he left Liverpool, until his retirement in 1954.

One of his sons, the scholar Eurys Rowlands, came to reside in Liverpool in the early 1980s.

Meuryn, as Robert John Rowlands was known in bardic circles, died on 2 November 1967.

The labour of love by John Evans

John Evans of Beaconsfield Street, Liverpool, was a lay preacher to the Welsh chapels of Liverpool and District for over fifty years and one of most remarkable hospital visitors of the 20th Century. Brought up in Liverpool, as a child and youth he attended the Welsh Calvinistic Methodist Chapel in Mulberry Street, and he remembered the congregation moving some three hundred yards to its new building in Chatham Street. He expressed an interest in preaching as early as 1870, but the chapel elders were not encouraging. He never surrendered his ambition, and some twelve years later they changed their stance. He proved to be a faithful, conscientious person, though he never possessed outstanding gifts as a communicator. His contribution to the Welsh Chapels of Liverpool and District was valuable, but his greatest contribution was as a visitor to the Welsh patients in the city's hospitals.

He began his visiting in earnest once he retired from his office job. He visited day after day, offering the patients comfort in their native tongue and representing in his person the Calvinistic Methodist Chapel of Chatham Street. The work was done voluntarily and he kept a detailed record of every patient, their background and the churches they belonged to, and he was always willing to write letters on their behalf to their families.

I remember hearing John Evans and his hospital ministry from one who knew him well, Miss Laura M Jones. She called him 'Uncle John' and he used to visit her home in Wavertree. She told me of his caring personality and of his sympathy for the sick amongst the Welsh, residing in Wales but who came for treatment to the Liverpool hospitals, as well as those Welsh people who resided in Liverpool. It is reckoned that he visited over ten thousand Welsh-speaking patients at least once and, in some cases, on numerous occasions. His care and concern were unceasing.

John Evans died on 12 June 1921, but others have kept his ministry alive up to the present, though since 1984 we have a full-time chaplain for the Merseyside Welsh, concentrating in particular on hospital patients.

■ *Miss Laura Myfanwy Jones (1890-1993)*

Meinwen Rees

Welsh League of Youth

The establishment of *URDD Gobaith Cymru* (Welsh League of Youth) by Sir Ifan ab Owen Edwards (1895-1970) in 1922 was a notable event, for the movement has become an integral part of the lives of young people who are enticed by Welsh culture. Ifan ab Owen Edwards had a close connection with the Merseyside Welsh, for his bride-to-be in 1922 was Eirys Mary Lloyd Phillips of Liverpool, a member of a devout Welsh Presbyterian family attending Princes Road Welsh Chapel. They married at Princes Road on 18 July 1923, lived at Neuadd Wen, Llanuwchllyn until 1930, and then resided in Aberystwyth. Two sons were born to them, Owen (a notable broadcaster) and Prys (an architect of flair and imagination).

Urdd Gobaith Cymru has played, and still plays, a role on Merseyside. In the early years Merseyside always sent a few representatives to the Council of the Welsh League of Youth. They included the Reverend W A Lewis of Sheil Road, and Mr Phillip H Jones of Birkenhead. Appeals for financial support always found supporters, like the Welsh Independents in Liverpool, and in an earlier period John Richard Jones of Cintra, Menlove Avenue. In the post-war period (from 1945-1975) the URDD had at least five Aelwydydd (Hearths) on Merseyside and the annual Eisteddfod was the climax of each centre's activities.

E. Emrys Jones

■ *Princes Road Presbyterian Church of Wales where the wedding was held in July 1923.*

Retirement of Captain Robert Parry

Captain Robert Parry served with distinction as Deputy Harbour Master of the Port of Liverpool. A native of Moelfre, Anglesey, he came to Liverpool as a young lad to work for the Mersey Docks and Harbour Board. As a sixteen year old he joined the Liverpool Pilot Scheme as an apprentice and, after completing his course, he served the American Line as a special steam pilot.

For many years he was extremely successful as a pilot bringing in the large steamers to Liverpool without a single accident. Parry was made Dock Master and later became Chief Deputy Harbour Master for the Port of Liverpool, one of the world's busiest and most important shipping ports. He retired in 1923 and with his wife, moved back to Anglesey, settling at Porth Llechog near Amlwch.

He died on 1 May 1932, after undergoing an operation at the home of his son, Dr J Rhynland Parry, at Finchley in London. The funeral was held at Amlwch Cemetery on May 4th with the Reverend D Cwyfan Hughes officiating.

The Gladstone Dock seen from the air during the time Captain Robert Parry served as Chief Deputy Harbour Master.

An Aerial photograph showing the approach to the city from the River Mersey.

The Welsh of Wigan

The Welsh flocked to Wigan early in the 19th Century and by the 1840s they had a flourishing chapel. This chapel, which was interdenominational, suffered from a clash of personalities and the spectre of denominationalism destroyed the community. Two chapels came into existence. In time, the Independent Chapel closed but the Welsh Calvinistic Methodist Chapel survived for generations. The first chapel, in Greenough Street, was opened in 1875 and the second in 1903. By 1924, there were sixty-one members and another sixty-nine adherents. The Sunday School was active with thirty-six members.

The chapel had a remarkable leader in John Williams of 23 Greenough Street. Elected an elder in 1878, he remained able and enthusiastic until his death in October 1925, a period of forty-seven years. He was elected Moderator of the Liverpool Presbytery in 1912. John Williams and his wife Ann were an exceptional couple: loyal, faithful and totally committed.

Wigan Pier

It has been redeveloped to include a Heritage Centre. It was extended in 1996, with the addition of an Art Gallery, given a generous grant by the National Lottery.

Population

According to the 1991 census: 84,700.

History

Wigan in Roman times was the site of the Roman garrison *Coccium*. It became, in the Middle Ages, an important trading centre and the Industrial Revolution changed the whole area. Coalmining became a key industry and the Welsh flocked to the settlements in the area, such as *Bryn* (Hill) and Ashton-in-Makerfield as well as Wigan itself. Rugby became a passion in Wigan and brought Welsh players to the town.

A glimpse of John Saunders Lewis of Liscard, Wallasey

■ *J. Saunders Lewis in his military attire*

This remarkable polymath was born in 1893 at Wallasey to a notable Calvinistic Methodist family. His father, Reverend Lodwig Lewis, ministered at Seacombe, his grandfather, Reverend Dr Owen Thomas was at Princes Road, and his great-grandfather, William Roberts, was at Amlwch. He was educated privately at first, then at Liscard High School for Boys, and the University of Liverpool, where he studied French and English, completing an MA aswell before moving to Wales in 1922.

England. He also found a spiritual corollary to this political stand, reflecting his Calvinistic background in the internationalism of the Catholic Church, which he joined in 1932. His Irish-Merseyside born wife, Margaret Gilchrist, was an obvious influence on this decision of his, which disturbed many of his contemporaries on Merseyside.

■ *The home of Saunders Lewis in Liscard (6 Wilton Street) where a plaque was placed on 25 February 2001 by the Merseyside Welsh Heritage Society.*

■ *The grave of the parents of Saunders Lewis, Reverend Lodwig Lewis and Mrs Mary Lewis at Anfield Cemetary*

In 1925 he helped to establish Plaid Cymru, the Welsh Nationalist Party, serving as its President from 1926-1939. He saw the Welsh nation in a European context rather than as an appendage to

Today Saunders Lewis is considered to be Wales's greatest dramatist. His plays (he published seventeen between 1936 and 1980) drew upon medieval Welsh literature and history; *Siwan* (1956), one of his classics, translated by Emyr Humphreys, can be read in ***Presenting Saunders Lewis*** (edited by Alun R Jones and Gwyn Thomas, University of Wales Press, Cardiff, 1992 [3rd edition]).

T J Hughes takes the initiative

In 1926 the spacious Audley House in London Road was vacant as the Owen Owen Company had moved to Clayton Square. Mr Duncan Norman, managing director, decided to contact another draper in the London Road area, T J Hughes, whose own business in Norton Street, needed larger premises.

■ *The famous TJ Hughes shop in London Road*

In 1926 the deal was clinched. It was agreed that T J Hughes, the enterprising Welshman, would sell his business to a small private company, to be known as T J Hughes & Co Ltd of which he should be the sole managing director, that Mr Duncan Norman, son-in-law of the late Owen Owen would become chairman and the only other director, and that this company should move into Audley House. On 7 October 1927, the reconstituted company opened for business and a new era for T J Hughes and his staff of two hundred (mostly Welshmen and women) had begun.

T J Hughes and Duncan Norman used to spend alternate Saturday afternoons together. They would meet in the city and then walk all the way to Anfield to watch Liverpool at home. They watched the game from immediately behind the goal because T J Hughes greatly admired Liverpool's fullback, 'Parson' Jackson and the moral example he set the rest of his team. It was Jackson's style of football and T J Hughes's upbringing within the Presbyterian Church of Wales in the city, which ultimately influenced his allegiance to Liverpool Football Club.

A Sunday School stalwart

On 29 September 1927 at 20 Wylfa Road, Anfield, Mr John Roberts died at the age of fifty-six. He was the son of William and Mary Roberts of Picton near Ffynnongroyw, became a member of the Fitzclarence Welsh Calvinistic Methodist Chapel, and in 1899 married Miss Alice Davies, a niece of the Reverend Howell Roberts (Hywel Tudur), of Clynnog. They became parents to five children, all who became involved in the lives of their communities and their chapels. The eldest was Howell (he became an elder at the Welsh Calvinistic Methodist Chapel in Waterloo), and the others were Trevor (a fine singer), Ceri, Gwyneth, and Arthur who lives in Roby and attends Bethel Welsh Presbyterian Chapel, Heathfield Road, Liverpool.

John Roberts worked for the builder John Williams, of Collingwood Street, for twenty-five years, and he was highly regarded as an honest and skilled craftsman. In 1915 the family moved to Anfield and became members of Bethlehem Douglas Road Welsh Presbyterian Chapel where John became a highly competent Sunday School teacher. He was very cultured in music and literature.

John was a great friend of R W Roberts (Arfonog) and J J Parry, two of the elders of Douglas Road Presbyterian Church of Wales.

The Sunday School movement

Though the Sunday School movement began within the Established Church, the Anglican Church failed to grasp the significance of the movement. The Calvanistic Methodists realised the opportunities presented, and hence Nonconformity rather than the Established Church played the major part in shaping Welsh education. Indeed the Sunday School became one of the outstanding institutions of teaching — instructing children to read and write and helping adults like John Roberts and Arfonog to reason and discuss serious theological and contemporary themes in the nineteenth century and up to the second world war. The Sunday School proved itself a powerhouse in the Merseyside Welsh community and a vast amount of religious literature was produced to provide for the needs of children as well as adults.

The opening of a new Welsh Centre

■ *Heathfield Road Welsh Chapel*

On 27 March 1927 a new building was opened on the borders of Wavertree and Allerton in South Liverpool. The work of building this large campus began in the spring of 1925. It was a huge task to build two large schoolrooms, four other sizeable rooms, a large chapel to seat seven hundred and twenty people, and a caretaker's house. The chapel in Webster Road was vacated on 2 August 1925. For nearly a year, from 9 August 1925 to 18 July 1926, the congregation met for their Sunday services at Dudley Institute off Smithdown Road. Then, by 25 July 1926, the large schoolroom facing Auckland Road had been completed, and on 27 March 1927 the chapel itself was opened. The meetings to open the new centre stretched for days, until April 3rd. In the grounds of the chapel the large caretaker's house was built mainly by volunteers from the building industry, members of the Church who gave freely of their time and energy. The whole project came to the sum of £27,000 and, even six years later, there still remained a debt of £4,000. But the Welsh Presbyterians of Heathfield Road cleared the sum. That called for a great deal of effort, a large Bazaar at St George's Hall, and the generosity of countless people.

Sefton Park, home to the last National Eisteddfod of Wales held in Liverpool in 1929

■ *A momento of the National Eisteddfod of Wales in Liverpool*

The Liverpool Welsh were extremely fortunate when they decided in 1928 to prepare for the National Eisteddfod of Wales to be held at Sefton Park in a year's time. This park covers three hundred and eighty-seven acres and there one always feels in the heart of the country. It was planned on the grand scale when the Corporation purchased the land from Lord Sefton in 1865. In area it rivals London's Hyde Park and consists of undulating ground traversed by two delightful valleys with a five acre lake fed by the stream Little Jordan, so named by the 16th Century Puritans who came from Bolton to live in the area.

Sefton Park has catered well for the large Welsh community that has long dwelt near it, and the coming of the National Eisteddfod in 1929 gave the Welsh a great sense of civic pride. The media as well as some city councillors have suggested that the National Eisteddfod should come back to Liverpool in 2007 when the city will be celebrating its Charter, given by King John in 1207. The National Eisteddfod has grown since 1929 and even Sefton Park would find it difficult to cater for all the different events, whilst also providing the necessary huge car park.

■ *Vaughan Jones of Bootle who did so much for the 1929 Eisteddfod*

The birth of Emrys Roberts of Llangadfan and Liverpool

Emrys Roberts was a poet, school-master, and Archdruid of the National Eisteddfod of Wales from 1987 until 1990. He was born on 3 September 1929. The family lived at 84 Royston Street, Liverpool 7, and Emrys was given his Christian name in admiration of the winning poet at the National Eisteddford of Wales in Liverpool in August 1929. Reverend D Emrys James, as he was to become, was better known as Dewi Emrys. He received his education at the primary school in Clint Road from 1933 until 1940, when his mother, Laura (née Jones), a native of Trawsfynydd, and his father, the poet J H Roberts (Monallt), decided to move to Penrhyndeudraeth. Emrys Roberts, after leaving college, taught in various schools from 1952 until 1961, and was then Headmaster of Banw School, Llangadfan from 1961 until his early retirement in 1986.

■ *Emrys Roberts as the Archdruid*

He is a prolific poet and author. His poetry has been presented in volumes such as *Y Gair yn y Glaw (The Word in Rain)* (1987), a number of children's books such as *Siani Ruban* (1973), and a delightful portrait of his father, *Monallt* (1978). Significant factors in his early years in Liverpool were the anti-Welsh feeling he often experienced as a child, and the thriving Welsh language community centred around the Welsh Presbyterian Chapel of Edge Lane.

Welsh Birkenhead actress

■ *Miss Megan R Thomas*

Megan R Thomas made her first appearance in front of the footlights when she was at junior school, and took leading parts in the productions of the Woodchurch Road Society, and was one of the most prominent performers in one of the casts entered by the Liverpool Welsh Players for the National Eisteddfod of Wales one-act play contest at Fishguard in 1936. Though a very versatile actress, Megan was always praised by the critics in the weekly Merseyside Welsh newspaper, *Y Brython* for her parts in straight comedies and farce. She also served for years as the Honorary Treasurer for the Liverpool Welsh Players, and it was in 1930 that she became a highly praised actress among Merseyside Welsh.

One of the outstanding Welsh amateur actresses of the 1930s was Megan R Thomas, the daughter of Mr and Mrs Ifan Thomas of Melrose, 61 North Road, Devonshire Park, Birkenhead, and sister of the Welsh children's writer, Jennie Thomas. Her father, a native of Anglesey, was a pioneer of Welsh drama on Merseyside, being closely associated with the Woodchurch Road Welsh Presbyterian Amateur Society from 1908 (when he was elected an elder) until his death in 1935. He was also closely associated with the flourishing Liverpool Welsh Dramatic Society.

■ *Her sister Miss Jennie Thomas*

Pedrog at the unveiling of a memorial to the authors of the Welsh National Anthem

The Welsh National Anthem, *Hen Wlad Fy Nhadau*, is an excellent work, full of passion. It has been recognised as a National Anthem since 1899, and has captured the hearts of all Welsh men and women, whether living in Wales or in exile on Merseyside.

■ *Reverend J O Williams*

On Wednesday, 23 July 1930, at Ynysangharad Park, Pontypridd, a memorial was unveiled in memory of Evan James (Ieuan ap Iago: 1809-1878), the writer of the words, and of his son, James James (1832-1902), who was responsible for the music. The dedication of the memorial was in the capable hands of the Reverend J O Williams (Pedrog) of Liverpool who praised the glorious wedding of poetry and music which brought the national anthem into existence. After being sung and played many times by the Jameses, it was sung publicly for the time in the schoolroom of the Welsh Calvinistic Methodist Chapel in Maesteg. James James sang it in 1857 at an eisteddfod at Pontypridd and it was sung at the 1884 National Eisteddfod in Liverpool.

Hen Wlad Fy Nhadau (Land Of My Fathers)

1

Mae hen wlad fy nhadau yn annwyl i mi,
Gwlad beirdd a chantorion, enwogion o fri;
Ei gwrol ryfelwyr, gwladgarwyr tra mâd,
Tros ryddid gollasant eu gwaed.

Cydgan:
Gwlad, Gwlad, pleidiol wyf i'm gwlad.
Tra môr yn fur i'r bur hoff bau,
O bydded i'r hen iaith barhau.

2.

Hen Gymru fynyddig, paradwys y bardd,
Pob dyffryn, pob clogwyn i'm golwg sydd hardd;
Trwy deimlad gwladgarol, mor swynol yw si
Ei nentydd, afonydd, i mi.

3.

Os treisiodd y gelyn fy ngwlad tan ei droed,
Mae hen iaith y Cymry mor fyw ag erioed,
Ni luddiwyd yr awen gan erchyll law brad,
Na thelyn berseiniol fy ngwlad.

Evan James

1.

The land of my fathers, the land of my choice,
The land in which poets and minstrels rejoice;
The land whose stern warriors were true to the core,
While bleeding for freedom of yore.

Chorus:
Wales! Wales! fav'rite land of Wales!
While sea her wall, may naught befall
To mar the old language of Wales.

2.

Old mountainous Cambria, the Eden of bards,
Each hill and each valley, excite my regards;
To the ears of her patriots how charming still seems
The music that flows in her streams.

3.

My country tho' crushed by a hostile array,
The language of Cambria lives out to this day;
The muse has eluded the traitors' foul knives,
The harp of my country survives.

Ebeneser Thomas (Eben Fardd)

■ *The National Anthem and a translation of it*

A knighthood to a Liverpudlian administrator

Sir David J Owen had a brilliant career. He was born in Liverpool in 1874. His father, Reverend R Ceinwenydd Owen, was a poet, and assisted the missionary work of Princes Road Welsh Calvinistic Methodist Chapel during the Ministry of the Reverend Dr Owen Thomas. The son never forgot his debt to this Liverpool Welsh background. Educated at the Liverpool Institute, he entered the service of the Mersey Docks and Harbour Board, then under the management of Miles Kirk-Burton, he rose to be an Assistant Committee Clerk. At the age of thirty (in 1904), he transferred as Manager and Secretary to Messrs Paul Bros, the flour millers of Birkenhead. However, his aptitude for dock management led to his appointment as Manager of the Goole Docks.

Then in 1915 David J Owen was appointed to a very important and demanding post as General Manager of the Belfast Harbour Commission, but he had the qualities which enabled him to carry out his duties in that position with great success. After seven years this led to his appointment as the General Manager to the Port of London Authority. Thanks to his genius, London became Britain's foremost port. Between 1922 and 1936, over £7,000,000 was spent on the improvement of the London Docklands before the Port of London Authority embarked upon a development scheme in connection with the Royal Victoria Dock, at an additional cost of £2,000,000.

As an administrator Owen was completely in a class of his own. The savings he achieved in administration and work extensions enabled the Authority to reduce their charges to the extend of nearly £1,000,000 per annum, as compared with 1922 when he took over, and it was largely due to this fact that the trade of the Port of London in the 1920s and 1930s increased by leaps and bounds, so that by 1937 the total exceeded that of the two next largest ports in the United Kingdom.

Like his father, he had ink in his blood. His publications include *A Short History of the Port of Belfast, A History of Belfast and The Port of London – Yesterday and Today.*

R W Pritchard: leader of the Welsh of Runcorn

◀ *The Welsh Chapel of Rutland Street which closed its doors on 4 March 2001*

R W Pritchard helped to maintain Welsh life in Runcorn for over fifty years. Born in 1848 in the Llŷn Peninsula, he came to Runcorn in 1872, where he remained for the rest of his life. Pritchard became extremely active in the life of the Runcorn Welsh community and especially in the life of the Welsh Calvinistic Methodist Chapel in Rutland Street. In 1888 he and Evan Williams were elected as elders, and he became Treasurer of the chapel until the end of 1929 when his son, John Pritchard, undertook the task.

R W Pritchard was a softly spoken, placid individual but who had strong convictions with regard to the need for Welsh Christianity for Welsh-speaking exiles. He was regarded as one of the most generous benefactors of the Runcorn Welsh community.

He died on 20 July 1932 at his home, 10 Brackley Street (a street in which other leaders of the Welsh chapels, such as John Wiliams, a native of Amlwch elected an elder in 1862, resided) and he was laid to rest in

E. Emrys Jones

■ *Widnes Town Hall where the well attended Runcorn-Widnes Eisteddfod was held in the inter-war years*

Greenway Road Cemetery. A Memorial Service was held for this remarkable Welsh Presbyterian on 7 August 1932, when a large gathering filled the Welsh chapel to listen to the tribute of their former minister, Reverend J H Hughes of Ellesmere Port, who had been the Minister at Runcorn for twenty-one years, from 1894 until 1915. The historian J Hughes Morris, in his second volume on the History of Liverpool Welsh Calvinistic Methodism, published in Welsh (see ***Hanes Methodistiaeth Liverpool***, Bootle 1932) paid this glowing tribute:

"Some of the members showed remarkable faithfulness for many years, and this history would not be complete without a special reference to the faithful and righteous elder, R W Pritchard and his wife – both are around till today, but now in great age and infirm. For nearly fifty years they have given sterling service to the cause, quietly and readily, no one knows how much they have done but the Lord of the Gospel who owes the work?"

A very fitting tribute from the pen of a minister who knew him over the years.

Elizabeth Ann Roberts: a truly spiritual individual

Elizabeth Ann Roberts was a devotional and influential member in the life of the Presbyterian Church of Wales in Princes Road, Liverpool. She was born in 1859 at Swansea, the daughter of Mr D Rees and his wife. Her parents moved to Liverpool when she was a baby, to keep a ship chandler's shop.

She had a very caring home background and attended the Welsh Independent Chapel at Grove Street. She married David Roberts, a member of Princes Road Chapel and became a member. A number of children were born to them, and she was well supported by her daughter Mrs Cledwyn Hughes, of Croxteth Road, and her son, Mr Arthur Roberts of Ohio, USA.

Mrs Elizabeth Ann Roberts was a devout person who had a gift of grace for the devotional and the spiritual. She read the Bible daily and had a very high regard for all the notable ministers who served Princes Road from the days of Dr Owen Thomas, Dr John Williams and Reverend Howell Harris Hughes to those of Reverend Griffith Rees. She was a gentlewoman in the Welsh settlement of Sefton Park and a peacemaker in her spirit. She passed on to glory at 36 Croxteth Road, Liverpool on 8 June 1932 and the funeral took place at Smithdown Road Cemetery with the Reverend Griffith Rees and the Reverend R J Williams officiating.

Preaching on Merseyside

No society in the twentieth century in any nation under the sun was treated to better preaching than the Merseyside Welsh. We may note the following names from among the Welsh Independents: Oldfield Davies, Wallasey; RJ Môn Hughes, Birkenhead; D Hughson Jones, Park Road; SB Jones, Great Mersey Street, J Pryce Davies, Bootle; D Kemes Lewis, Allerton, and from among the Presbyterians or Welsh Calvanistic Methodists Dr John Williams, Princes Road; Llewelyn Lloyd, Chatham Street; Griffith Rees, Princes Road; Easter Ellis, Walton Park; William Davies and D Tudor Jones, Stanley Road; Iorwerth Jones Owen, Parkfield; G Tudor Owen, Douglas Road and Cledwyn Griffiths, Anfield and Ifor Oswy Davies, Princes Road. The Welsh Wesleyan Methodists had their pulpit giants on Merseyside in the personalities of E Tegla Davies; D Tecwyn Evans; J Roger Jones and the Welsh Baptists in the powerful ministeries of Glyn Davies Jones; W Lloyd Williams and I Cyril John. What a list and what a privilege to those who attended the weekly services

Plaid Cymru's presence in the North West

■ *Three of the most well known Welsh Nationalists of the 1930s. From left to right: Reverend Lewis Valentine, Llandudno, Saunders Lewis, Swansea and DJ Williams, Fishguard.*

The tenth Regional Committee for Plaid Cymru was established in Liverpool in 1933 and encompassed the North West. J E Jones, the ever-active General Secretary, came to speak and the officers were elected. The President, Gwilym R Jones, was the editor of the weekly newspaper *Y Brython*. The Treasurer, H Arthur Jones, came from Manchester, and the Secretary, R Gordon Williams, taught in Ashton-in-Makerfield. The Executive included J R Morris, a bookseller from Renshaw Street, the poet William Morgan (Collwyn), the science writer O E Roberts, Miss Olwen Ellis, who worked for years at Gee Press, Denbigh, and Mrs Llinos (née Roberts), a native of Pen-y-groes in the Nantlle Valley. The two most notable people among them would be Mr and Mrs Eilian Roberts. They had a second home in Llaneilian, Anglesey, and he was a well-known accountant in Liverpool. Related by family ties to the President of the Party, Wallasey-born J Saunders Lewis, Eilian Roberts was a catalyst for the newly-established political party on Merseyside. It was he who persuaded Dr and Mrs H Francis Williams of Wallasey to be generous donors to Plaid Cymru.

The efforts of Hugh Evans as an author

Hugh Evans (1854-1934) was the founder of the well-known Welsh publishing and printing establishment, Messrs Hugh Evans and Sons Ltd, of Stanley Road, Bootle. His work was carried on by his sons, E Meirion Evans and Howell Evans, and then by his grandchildren Bronwen Evans and Alun Evans. Their contribution to Welsh literature was immense.

Hugh Evans wrote a book called **Cwm Eithin** which was later translated into English by E Morgan Humphreys, under the title **Gorse Glen**, and has become a classic. It gives a marvellous insight into the life of the Welsh people in the Cerrigydrudion area in the 19th

Century before the coming of mechanisation and technology. Later, Hugh Evans wrote a book called **Y Tylwyth Teg,** *(The Fairies),* a very endearing collection of Welsh fairy tales and folklore published in a delightful edition by the Brython Press of Stanley Road in 1935. **Y Tylwyth Teg** did not become a classic like **Cwm Eithin**, but for its binding alone it deserves to be in the collection of every Welsh bibliophile.

Hugh Evans died at Pen-y-bryn, Cynwyd near Corwen on 30 June 1934 and was buried at Longmoor Lane Cemetery, Kirkdale, Liverpool.

The site of the Brython Press in Stanley Road

Owain Cadwaladr Roberts as High Sheriff

Owain Cadwaladr Roberts was born in Bethesda, Caernarfonshire, son of Cadwaladr and Elisabeth Roberts. He was educated at the local primary school of Carneddi and left at fourteen years of age to seek his fortune in Liverpool. He came to live with his uncle, R O Roberts (of 263 Bedford Road, Bootle) who was an elder in Crosshall Street Welsh Presbyterian Chapel from 1880 until its closure in 1920. The youngster went to work with the same builders' merchants which had trained J W Jones.

At the age of twenty-one Owain decided to enter the building industry with R O Roberts and his uncle's brother-in-law. Later he became a partner with Liverpool Welsh builders John Jones, of Mayfield, and John Hughes, of Monevion, and with the Costain Company.

Owain C Roberts lived at Prenton on Merseyside during his first marriage. He lost his wife at the birth of a child who also died. He married again, his second wife being Florence Louisa from Wallasey and a son, Eldred Owen Roberts, was born to them. A street in Childwall built by O C Roberts and his partners was named Eldred Road, and it is still there. He moved to Menlove Avenue and built a house called *Bryntirion*. The name is still at the entrance to the house.

Later Owain moved to London to continue building and became extremely successful on the Kenton estate. After his second marriage ended, he wedded Mary Myfanwy (née Williams), whose brother, Llywelyn Williams, ministered for a while at New Brighton. After their spell in London he and his third wife lived in Wales, at Plas y Bryn, Bontnewydd near Caernarfon, and also at the Llanfair Hall Estate between Caernarfon and Port Dinorwic. There he died in 1946 and was laid to rest at Coetmor Cemetery in Bethesda. O C Roberts was the High Sheriff of Caernarfonshire in 1935 and in his day was one of the most successful Liverpool Welsh builders.

Death of a Liverpool ship-owner

Mr Richard Hughes, who died as his residence in the seaside village of Abersoch, Caernarfonshire in 1936, was the founder of the well-known Liverpool firm of ship-owners, Messrs Richard Hughes and Company. He was seventy-eight years of age and had spent the major part of his life in Liverpool, retiring from business in 1931.

A native of Gronant, near Prestatyn, Richard Hughes came to Liverpool before he was fourteen years of age, and started to work for the Welsh firm of Messrs R & D Jones. They were

Richard Hughes lived for a time at Bryn Coch Hall, near the market town of Mold. He was made a magistrate for Flintshire and had a great love of Liverpool as well as Flintshire and later Abersoch. He was survived by his daughter, Mrs Wallace Jones, the wife of Dr H Wallace Jones of Rodney Street, Liverpool.

◄ The Queen Mary

ship-owners and he soon climbed the greasy pole. He was so successful that by 1924 he could present his native village with an Institute and bowling green.

Gift of an organ

In 1936 Mr H Iorwerth Hughes, of Minffordd, Mossley Hall, presented to Glan y Mor Church in Llanddona, Anglesey, with a beautiful organ in memory of his father, Hugh Hughes of Kiimblerley Street, Liverpool and Benllech. Hugh was elected an elder in

(together with R Osborne Hughes, of Park Road, R E Jones of Beaumont Street, and Professor O Herbert Williams, FRCS, of Rodney Street), and in 1935 H Iorwerth Hughes followed in the footsteps of his father and brother.

■ *Professor O Herbert Williams*

O R Hughes and H Iorwerth Hughes were directors of Messrs Owens Peck and Company, timber merchants of Liverpool. I have very fond memories of Mrs O R Hughes when she lived in Green Lane. She was a very kind, considerate individual and was grateful for her long association with the Liverpool Welsh and proud of all that her husband's family did within the community.

Chatham Street Welsh Presbyterian Chapel in 1911, then in 1919 his son O R Hughes was elected an elder

A producer of Welsh plays

The Welsh Amateur Dramatic Society, known also as the Liverpool Welsh Players, were very fortunate in having as their producer Morris Jones of Kensington. Although comparatively young in years, by 1937 he already had a wide and varied career with a large number of amateur dramatic societies.

In the 1930s Morris Jones produced plays for the following societies in Liverpool: Edge Lane Welsh Presbyterian Church Amateur Dramatic Society, Mersey ADS, Automatic Telephone ADS, the Liverpool Technical College ADS, and the Liverpool Union of Boys' Clubs ADS. He also produced two plays for the Llanelly National Eisteddfod of 1936, namely **Yr Ymadawedig** (Stanley Houghton's *The Dear Departed*, translated by R E Jones) and **Y Bachgennyn Hwn** (Cedric Mount's *Twentieth Century Lullaby*, translated by the editor of the **Brython** newspaper, Gwilym R Jones.

■ *Mr Morrris Jones*

Morris Jones was an innovator and not afraid of experimenting with new ideas in stagecraft and dramatic techniques. He proved invaluable as a producer of Welsh plays.

The success of the Birkenhead Welsh Choral Union

Among the Merseyside Welsh Choirs of the inter-war years, one has to mention the Birkenhead Welsh Choral Union. It was trained and conducted by a very able musician, D R Jones, a compositor at a Birkenhead newspaper office.

The choir won a large number of trophies and prizes in important choral contests all over North Wales and Merseyside, including the second choral competition at the National Eisteddfod of Wales. In the 1920s, D R Jones frequently appeared in the lists of successful baritones at most of the Merseyside Eisteddfodau as well as at the Provincial Eisteddfodau of Wales.

The choir often won the first prize for a rendering of *Y Storm (The Storm)*, from the work of Dr Joseph Parry. The Birkenhead Welsh Choral Union was very popular in the Penllyn and Edeyrnion areas of Merionethshire as well as in the Vale of Clwyd. They regularly competed at the chief choral contest at Swan Lane Independent Chapel Eisteddfod in the town of Denbigh, and did so again in 1937.

E. Emrys Jones

■ *Bala, the heart of Penllyn and Edeyrnion*

Poet's remains under the stadium?

In 1938 the Liverpool Welsh poet, J H Roberts (Monallt) raised once again the question of the locality of the grave of Peter Jones (Pedr Fardd), the 19th Century Welsh poet and hymn writer of great distinction, who died in 1840. Pedr Fardd spent most of his life in Liverpool, including Orange Street, near Tithebarn Street Station, and was an elder at the old Pall Mall Calvinistic Chapel for forty years. Liverpool Welsh poets of the 1930s, such as Gwilym Deudraeth and Monallt, suggested that his last resting place was under the site of the Liverpool stadium. He had been buried in the cemetery of the church which was demolished to make room for that stadium, which became a mecca for boxing supporters like the late William Edwards, known by his bardic name of Gwilym Deudraeth. I am deeply disturbed that we do not know the whereabouts of

■ *J H Roberts*

the marvellous poet's grave and I feel that it is a sad reflection, especially upon the Presbyterian Church of Wales. We should do something soon in the Pall Mall area to remember the life and work of Pedr Fardd, and the publication of this book should inspire us to act within the next twelve months.

"He built half of Wallasey"

Moses Hughes, born in 1866 in Llanfairfechan, came as a lad of twelve to Seacombe to work for his uncle, Evan Hughes. He received his higher education at the Liverpool Institute, but in 1888 emigrated to New York. By 1895, however, he decided to return to Wallasey where he was to achieve his great ambition. Moses Hughes bought land and began building in what came to be called Garden Road and Seabank Road. In fact this was just the beginning. He built on a vast scale in Vaughan, Sandrock and Earlston Roads, as well as in Rake Lane. He then concentrated on Liscard, Seacombe, Seaforth and Crosby. His last big project was the Bayswater Road Estate in Wallasey.

Moses Hughes was an influential person within the Welsh Wesleyan Methodist Church, holding a large number of important offices. He was also a prominent figure in the wider Welsh Community of Merseyside until his death in 1939. No wonder the heading for his obituary in the local paper proclaimed, "...he built half of Wallasey". It was true.

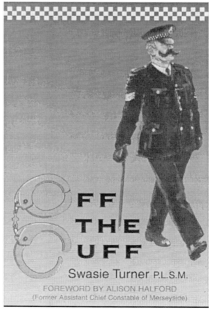

■ *The autobiography of Swasie Turner, who served as a police sargeant in Wallasey and who has learnt Welsh. He is one of the great characters of present day Merseyside*

The life and work of Dr William Robert Williams

Dr William Robert Williams was a well-known Liverpool Welsh surgeon. He was born in Warrington on 24 April 1898, the eldest son of William Thomas Williams and his wife Jane (née Jones). His father was a draper in the town and the family were loyal members of the Welsh Calvinistic Methodist Chapel in Warrington. His sister and her husband carried on the family tradition, and I remember well their tenderness in their home at Appleton, near Warrington.

Williams was educated at the Boterlic Grammar School, Warrington and the University Liverpool, gaining the Derby Exhibition in Clinical Medicine and the Robert Gee Fellowship in Anatomy.

Dr Williams served as House Surgeon at Southern Hospital, and as Surgical Registrar and Tutor at the Royal Infirmary. He also was appointed Demonstrator of Anatomy at the University. Dr Williams became surgeon in charge of the Southern Hospital Outpatients' Department from 1924 until his premature death in 1940. He acted as Surgeon of the Heart Hospital in Liverpool from 1934, as well as being Honorary Surgeon to the Prince Edward Memorial Hospital in Rhyl and the Dolgellau Hospital.

He married Margaret Enid Williams from Llandudno in 1924 and a son and daughter were born to them. Dr Williams was an extremely lovable surgeon who became a great friend to his patients. He was highly talented at diagnosis, and articles written by him appeared in the journal, *Lancet* for 1925 and 1927.

Dr Williams had numerous qualifications. He gained MB and ChB in 1919, then FRCS, MRCS and LRCP in 1920, another FRCS in 1924, and FRCP (Edinburgh) in 1929.

He gave his best to the Welsh Presbyterian Chapel at Belvedere Road and was elected an elder in 1929. Four others were elected the same time as him, namely W P Bryan of Kinnaird Street, O C Roberts of Menlove Avenue, W D Simon of Thackeray Street, and Mrs E R Jones, Briarley (the daughter of an elder of an earlier period, John Thomas of Waverley Road), the first woman to be given such responsibility in any of Liverpool's Welsh Presbyterian Chapels.

Dr Williams lived in Druids Cross Road in Calderstones, and gave his house the Welsh name of Pentan (Hearth). He died on 27 June 1940, a year in which many leaders of the Welsh Community on Merseyside were called to higher service.

Merseyside Blitz

1941 was a bitter year for Merseyside because of the bombing. Eighteen thousand, eight hundred and forty houses were damaged, and ten thousand, eight hundred and forty destroyed. On 14 May 1941, one thousand dead were given a mass burial in a common grave at Anfield Cemetery. In Bootle a sizeable number of the houses were damaged or destroyed and Stanley Road Welsh Presbyterian Chapel as well as Marsh Lane Welsh Independent Chapel suffered damage.

*"Wake up girl, the siren's going
Best take to the shelters tonight
I can hear Gerry over the city
And the sky's like bonfire night."*

The above verse by Brenda Walker from the poem "*This Game of War,*
published in *Both Sides of the River:
Merseyside in Poetry and Prose,*
compiled and Edited by Gladys Mary Coles (Headland Publications, 1993, 188), sums up the reality on Merseyside, and so does the following:

*"One day a German plane landed
in a field by the side of the road,
and when the pilot got out
I could see he was just like Dad."*
Brenda Walker's final verse says it all:

*"I was too young to understand what I saw,
too young to say what I thought,
I just knew they'd got it wrong
this game of war."*

Many felt like Brenda Walker,

*"I just knew they'd got it wrong
this game of war."*

CHILDREN
of the
BLITZ
by KEN BLASBERY

■ *A dramatic account of Ken Blasbery's experience as a schoolboy during the bombardment endured by the inhabitants of Merseyside during the second world war.*

A unique ministry in Liverpool

The Reverend John Hughes Morris (1870-1953) had a unique ministry in Liverpool. He served in the office of the Presbyterian Church of Wales Foreign Mission at Falkner Street from 1892 to 1949, and by 1942 he had been an ordained minister for over forty years. J Hughes Morris never took charge of a church but lived with his sister at 96 Edge Lane, attending the Welsh Chapel of Edge Lane. His education was meagre, mainly at Chatsworth Street School, but he could write in both languages with style. He wrote in Welsh two extremely important volumes on the history of the Presbyterian Church of Wales. The first volume, under the title

■ *Chatsworth Primary School, one of Liverpool's first Board Schools, where the Reverend J Hughes Morris received his education*

Hanes Methodistiaeth Liverpool, was published in 1929 and the second volume, under the same title, *History of Methodist in Liverpool,* saw the light of day in 1932. He also wrote extensively on the missionary work in North East India, and edited the Welsh language monthly magazine ***Y Cenhadwr,*** *(The Missionary)* from 1922 until 1949, as well as the English language edition called ***Glad Tidings.***

■ *Ministers and elders who attended the General Assembly of the Presbyterian Church of Wales at Edge Lane Chapel in 1947*

Five Welsh Ministerial Students among the Presbyterians of Merseyside

Merseyside Welsh Presbyterians had a great deal to celebrate in 1943 for they had five young men training for the Christian Ministry. All of them had already spent some years in preparation and were now on the threshold of being called to pastorates in Wales, or among the Welsh

■ *JR Davies, an elder in Heathfield Road, father of Aled Davies and father-in-law of Trebor Mai Thomas*

communities in England. E Ffrancon Davies, of 7 Ripon Road, Wallasey, was at the United Theological College, Aberystwyth, while H Godfrey Jones, of 4 Truro Road, Liverpool 15, and Trevor Davies Jones, of 23 Beckenham Avenue, Liverpool 15, were both at Westminster College, Cambridge. They had already gained degrees in Arts and Theology.

Llywelyn Hughes of Princes Road Chapel was at the University of Wales, Bangor, as was G Meirion Williams, of 2 Newlyn Avenue, Litherland, a product of Stanley Road, Bootle, Presbyterian Church of Wales. Each had remarkable scholarly ministers to encourage them. Of the five, only two remain today in the ranks of the retired Presbyterian ministers, Reverend Ffrancon Davies (ordained in 1943) at Kenfig Hall, near Bridgend in Glamorganshire, and Reverend Trefor Davies Jones (ordained in 1944), who lives at Cerrig-mân near Amlwch in Anglesey. Two years earlier three young men had been ordained as Ministers of Religion, namely Aled Davies BA, 44 Dovedale Road and a product of Heathfield Road Welsh Chapel (who began his ministry in Aberdeen), Trebor Mai Thomas BA BD, from Stanley Road Welsh Chapel and who married Aled's sisters, Nancy Davies and began as a missionary in Shillong, North East India and W Bryn Roberts BA, (78 Higher John Street, Blackburn) and a product of the Welsh Chapel in Blackburn and who began as a minister at Bwlchgwyn outside Wrexham.

The life of the Reverend Dr J G Moelwyn Hughes

John Gruffydd Moelwyn Hughes (1866-1944) was a native of the village of Tanygrisiau, near Blaenau Ffestiniog. He began his career as Clerk to the budding politician David Lloyd George, a post he filled for four years at the office in Porthmadog before he entered various colleges. He was educated at Clynnog, Bangor, Bala and later the University of Leipzig from where he graduated with an MA and PhD.

Ordained in 1894, he ministered at Neath and Cardigan, and at Parkfield Welsh Chapel, Birkenhead from 1917 to his retirement in 1936. That year he was inducted as Moderator of the General Assembly of the Presbyterian Church of Wales at Abergele and gave a powerful address which upset many of the Presbyterians as he showed his allegiance to the Labour Party.

A powerful and outspoken preacher, he was often sought as a *Cyrddau Mawr* (Special Meetings) preacher. His spectrum of talent included poetry, and he was one of the adjudicators of the Crown Competition at the 1931 National Eisteddfod of Wales held at Bangor.

■ *Dr J G Moelwyn Hughes with his elders in the 1920's*

Hew edited the Welsh Presbyterian monthly magazine **Y Drysorfa** (1934-1938) and was the author of a number of Welsh books including a volume of sermons in 1925 and a volume on **Addoli** (*Worship*) in 1935. His English book was **A New Method for the Study of the German Language**, *published in* 1922.

Dr J G Moelwyn Hughes died on 25 June 1944, a few months after his wife Myra (née Lewis), and they were both laid to rest at Llangadog in the Tywi Valley.

■ *Another era — in the 1930's*

The loss of John Meirion Evans of Rake Lane Chapel, New Brighton

The sudden death of a Presbyterian Church of Wales leader, born at Bala, was deeply felt on Merseyside. J Meirion Evans came to Liverpool when he was sixteen years of age, and settled in the Anfield area where there was a large Welsh settlement. He then moved to the Edge Lane area and attended Holt Road Chapel before they moved in 1900, some hundred yards to a large building in Edge Lane. He was elected an elder in 1920 but within two years he moved to 23, Kingsway Road Wallasey, where he was elected an elder in 1927 at the Welsh Chapel in rake Lane, New Brighton. Later he moved to live at 26 Mount Road, Wallasey.

An extraordinary individual he was always ready to serve, and was a regular visitor to the Welsh families and a remarkable teacher to his Sunday School class. Elected Moderator of the Liverpool Prebytery on 16 May 1945, he took up his office on 25 July. But he died suddenly when addressing the Chapel of Rake Lane, New Brighton on 23 August at the service to wish their minister a blessing as he left for a new pastorate and as he pointed out to the congregation the difficulties at the end of the Second World War for a Welsh minister on Merseyside. Rake Lane Welsh Chapel, New Brighton had in 1945, besides John Meirion Evans, four other elders, namely, the chemist Hywel D Williams of 227 Seaview Road (he later moved to Rhuddlan); R Leslie Davies, 25 Beverley Road, who took over as Treasurer from J M Evans; P Lloyd Edwards, 12 Treforris Road, Wallasey and E Lloyd Humphreys, the father of the present organist of Rake Lane, Goronwy Humphreys.

J M Evans held strong convictions and he exerted a great deal of influence in the first half of the 20th Century among the Merseyside Welsh.

The talented William Albert Williams

William Albert Williams was one of the most talented composers among the Liverpool Welsh, and in his short life, he contributed immensely. The son of a sea captain, Captain Richard Williams, and his wife Anne, both natives of Marianglas in Anglesey, he was born at Anfield on 16 January 1903. His father drowned when he was only three years of age, while his mother died when he was fifteen. He and his brother, who was to become Reverend Professor Harri Williams, were cared for by their mother's sister, Mrs Stanley Jones.

William Albert Williams became well known in Liverpool Welsh circles at the age of sixteen when he was appointed organist of Chatham Street Welsh Presbyterian Chapel and later he became organist at Douglas Road Welsh Presbyterian Chapel and the English Congregationalist Chapel of Great George Street. He was employed from the age of sixteen as a clerk, for the Liverpool City Corporation, and he spent his leisure hours receiving further tuition, writing on numerous subjects relating to music, in particular for the Welsh language newspapers, *Y Brython* and the *Cymro,* as well as competing regularly in the composition section of the National Eisteddfod of Wales.

He married Glenys Jones, a kind, lively female from Church Village, near Pontypridd in 1940 and she became a great help to him. Later she returned to Liverpool with her second husband, Reverend Dr H Islwyn Davies and I was privileged to become his friend and enjoy the fellowship of both of them.

■ *Great George's Street Congregationalist Chapel*

W Albert Williams died at Middlesex Hospital on 8 January 1946. It was a great loss to the Cardiganshire Education Authority, as he had been appointed their Music Organiser. His early death was a great blow to the Welsh of Liverpool and indeed, as John Hughes (1896-1968) of Dolgellau said, *"It meant also a great loss to Welsh music."*

Closure of a Welsh centre on the Wirral

One of the greatest failures of the Welsh in the Merseyside area was the failure to establish a strong and permanent presence in the town of Heswall in the heart of the Wirral peninsula. It is a thriving community and a number of Welsh-speaking individuals still live in the area in the year 2001. The Welsh Presbyterian Chapel was opened in 1933 as there were a number of Welsh speakers in Heswall and the surrounding villages. By 1941, however, they were in financial difficulties and it was then that they appealed to Presbytery for funds. These were granted, but by the beginning of 1947 it was obvious that the experiment had been a dismal failure. The Presbytery appointed three leaders to meet the Welsh men and women of Heswall and prepare a report.

R T Jones of Birkenhead and two ministers, Reverend R Emrys Evans and Reverend Llewelyn Jones, met at Heswall on 20 July and 7 September. They decided to recommend closure. The chief reason was lack of leaders. A number of leaders at Heswall had died in the war years and there was nobody willing to take responsibility. A familiar story.

Heswall is regarded as a healthy spot to live, and undoubtedly that is why the Royal Liverpool Children's Hospital and the Cleaver Sanatorium were built there. Both have been demolished and closed like the Welsh Chapel. So has the railway been closed, and although the Heswall Station was sold for housebuilding, the remainder is part of the popular Wirral Way long distance path.

One of the best places to see the green hills of Wales is from St Peter's Church where time is eternal. Not far from here, William of Orange is reputed to have had his horse shod at the village smithy before embarking from Hoylake for Ireland and the Battle of the Boyne over 300 years ago. He had spent the previous night at Gayton Hall, secluded among the trees, close today to Heswall Golf Club.

NHS begins care from cradle to grave

■ *Harry Evans*

One of Bevan's greatest supporters was Horace Evans (1903-1963) later Baron Evans of Merthyr Tudful, the eldest son of the Liverpool Welsh musician Harry Evans, and his wife, Edith Gwendolen (née Rees). Horace Evans became the physician to the Royal Family – to Queen Mary in 1946, to George VI in 1949 and to Queen Elizabeth in 1952, and they regarded him as their friend. He was a remarkable physician and was proud of the National Health Service.

The National Health Service came into existence on 5 July 1948, together with a national insurance scheme and other welfare systems dealing with the unemployed and the elderly. The service represented a personal triumph for a fireband Welsh Socialist, Aneurin Bevan, the Health Minister, and MP for Ebbw Vale. He faced powerful opposition from the British Medical Association and a large number of individual doctors when he began negotiations in 1947.

In 1929 he married Helen Aldwyth from Swansea and they had two daughters. The younger one died in tragic circumstances but I remember the elder as a student at the University of Wales, Aberystwyth in the late fifties.

■ *Liverpool Choral Union which established itself under the baton of Harry Evans*

The closure of Peel Road Welsh Chapel, Seaforth

The Peel Road Welsh Presbyterian Chapel had been one of the most outgoing, active chapels in North Liverpool, and I well remember, as a child in Cardiganshire, listening during a Sunday morning service to a visiting preacher from Cardigan, Reverend Curie Hughes. He was a first-class preacher who had ministered at Peel Road in the 1920s. Peel Road Chapel was renowned for its flourishing Sunday School, its active youth clubs and its children's meetings. After the First World War, decline set in as the Welsh settlement around the chapel began to disperse. They moved out to Waterloo, Crosby and Blundellsands. The Welsh ceased to move into the Peel Road area, the Liverpool Irish taking their place.

There were other unfavourable factors in addition to the demographic change. A dispute arose and many of the members left for other chapels. By 1939 there were only eighty-eight members left out of a total of three hundred and thirty-one, twenty-two years earlier. To complicate matters the building was hit by German bomb during the Second World War. A small group tried to keep the Welsh presence alive, but by 1949 they found it too hard and it was decided to close the Peel Road Chapel. The final service was held in June 1949.

E. Emrys Jones

■ *Stanley Road Welsh Presbyterian Chapel, Bootle where most of the Peel Road members were welcomed at the closure of their chapel in 1949*

Richard John Jones leaves Anfield for Bethesda

Richard John Jones was born in Llanfachreth, Anglesey on 14 January 1886 and after leaving school he moved to Deeside and then on to West Kirby. There in 1910 he married Elizabeth Thomas from the Bethesda area and they had five children, Olwen, Elma, Beth, Huw and Goronwy. They moved from Hoylake, which meant a great loss to the Welsh Community in West Kirby, to Anfield in 1914, and lived at Ince Avenue and then 129 Priory Road until 1950 when they moved to Gerlan, Bethesda. He died in 1972.

They became members of Bethlehem Chapel in Douglas Road and in 1928 he was elected an elder at the same time as William Jones of Valley Road, and W J Roberts of Moss Lane, elders of the chapel. He used to mention how he had been privileged to receive edification from four ministers, two fathers and two sons. At Abrim, Llanfachreth J E Jones (Dolfor) ministered, while his son Llywelyn Jones was at Douglas Road, and then when he arrived at Douglas Road he was received by the Reverend G Wynne Griffith, whilst at the end of his life he sat under the preaching of his son, Reverend Huw Wynne Griffith, at Seilo, Aberystwyth. Their home in Anfield was always open to the Welsh of the area, and R J Jones was for years the Secretary of the Douglas Road Chapel.

Five new elders were elected in 1938, DH Hughes, 52 Utting Avenue; O G Hughes, 20 Whinmore Road, Liverpool 12; Alun Jones, 49 Robarts Road (whose grave I saw on Easter Sunday 2001 when I visited Glanyrafon Parish Church between Corwen and Bala); R Alun Roberts, 16 College Avenue, Crosby (and today an elder in Bethania Waterloo Welsh Chapel in Crosby Road South) and WR Thomas, 131 Priory Road. The other outstanding elder was Dr TE Jones, Oakfield, who had been an elder since 1919. He died in 1947.

The life of Reverend Robert Richard Hughes, late of Chatham Street, Liverpool

Reverend Robert Richard Hughes was minister of the Presbyterian Church of Wales, Chatham Street, Liverpool from 1913 to 1922. Born on 2 January 1871 at Pont Myfyrian, a small cottage near the railway line not far from Brynsiencyn and Gaerwen, Anglesey, he was brought up in the chapel at Brynsiencyn during the ministry of Dr John Williams. Ordained in 1898, he ministered at Kingsland, Holyhead until he moved to Liverpool at the end of the summer of 1913 to be the minister of Chatham Street, residing at 129 Chatham Street.

The church membership rose to three hundred and thirty-two at the end of that year. A number of young people joined the church during the ministry of Richard Hughes, and this was most encouraging in a cause which had been deeply divided over the resignation of W O Jones. At the end of 1920 the membership had risen to three hundred and sixty-four, but one must remember that thirty members had joined after the closure of Victoria Chapel, Cross Hall Street. He was made Moderator of the Liverpool Presbytery in 1920.

He ended his relationship with the church in March 1922 when he received a call to Newborough, Anglesey, where he remained until he retired in 1947. In 1897 he had married Margaret Ann Lewis from Bootle, and a son and a daughter were born to them.

He was busy as a writer, and he is seen at his best in the biography of his old minister, Reverend Dr John Williams of Brynsiencyn, published by the Connexion in 1929. He mentions in the biography how he had promised a Liverpool Welsh businessman, Arthur Venmore, to write the biography and that he had received assistance from a number of Liverpool ministers. Mention is made of the Reverend H M Pugh, D Francis Roberts and T R Jones (Clwydydd) and, more than anyone else, of the Reverend John Owen (Anfield), *"...out of his huge resource of knowledge of the Connexion."*

Reverend R R Hughes died at Holyhead on 23 September 1951 and was laid to rest at Maeshyfryd Cemetery in the town.

The achievement of Owen Elias Roberts

Owen Elias Roberts was a scientist and author. Born in Llanystumdwy, Caernarfonshire on 19 June 1908, the son of William Roberts and Mary (née Jones Elias), he was educated at the Primary School, Llanystumdwy, the County School, Porthmadog and the Technical College, Liverpool. He was the Chief Medical Technician for the Liverpool Hospitals Laboratories from 1926 until his retirement in 1972, concentrating his skills at the Broadgreen Hospital whilst residing in Childwall.

During his period in Liverpool he became prominent as a writer. He frequently wrote to the local Welsh language journals, *Y Glannau* and *Y Bont,* and served on the Editorial Board of both. He wrote occasionally under the pseudonym Eifionydd.

He was elected an elder in the Welsh Presbyterian Chapel, Anfield Road in 1947, and later he became a member at the Heathfield Road church. Roberts was a prominent member of the Pastoral Committee of that Church when it extended an invitation to me to become their minister early in 1968.

Roberts won the Prose Medal at the National Eisteddfod of Wales on two

occasions. The first was at the National Eisteddford of Wales held at Aberystwyth in 1952 and was for a volume of essays or articles that had not been published. The result of that competition was the volume Cyfrinach Natur (The Secrets of Nature) which was published in 1953. At the National Eisteddford of Wales at Ystradgynlais

■ *O E Roberts and his wife Mrs Florence Roberts*

in 1954 he won again on a similar theme as at the Aberystwyth Eisteddford. The following year a volume called *Y Gŵr o Ystradgynlais ac Erthyglau Eraill,* (The man from Ystradgynlais and other Essays) appeared. He has been active writing biographies of scientists in the Welsh language. 'OE', as he was affectionately known, served as Honorary President of the Welsh Science Association from 1978 to 1980. He moved from Liverpool to Criccieth and he and his wife, Mrs Florence Roberts, then lived near their only daughter, Mrs Gwenan Richards and her family, at Radyr, a suburb of Cardiff, until his death in October 2000.

Pattern of a Welshwoman

■ *Elisabeth Watcyn Thomas*

When Mrs Elisabeth Watcyn Thomas died suddenly at Wrexham on 24 October 1953, the editor of the Welsh newspaper Y Faner, Gwilym R Jones, gave her the title of *"Pattern of a Welshwoman"*, in particular for her time in Liverpool. She was born at Cwm Cynllwyd, Llanuwchllyn, in Merionethshire, in 1887, and in 1915 married Dan Thomas. They lived at Kimberley Street and then Ducie Street, both in Liverpool, and her home was an open house to young people from Wales who attended the Welsh Presbyterian Chapel of Chatham Street, students from the area of every nationality, members of the Labour Party, as her husband was a prominent socialist, friends of her son Dewi and daughter Rhiannon, and individuals from her home territory who were visiting loved ones in local hospitals.

■ *Rhiannon and Gwynfor Evans*

Auntie Liz (as she was known) loved to welcome everyone, prepare meals and entertain those who came to Liverpool. *"Croeso"* (welcome) was always on her lips. It was a great loss when the family moved from Liverpool to Cardiff in 1937. She involved herself from 1939 until her death as Treasurer of the Welsh Peace Society, a movement in which her son-in-law, Gwynfor Evans, served as Secretary.

■ *Gwynfor Evans*

A Labour MP lectures at Bootle on Ishmael Jones (1794-1876)

In 1954, T W Jones, the Labour Member of Parliament for Merionethshire came to lecture to the Bootle Welsh Society on *'The original Ishmael Jones'*. T W Jones possessed a great deal of humour and he and his brother James Idwal Jones became Members of Parliament in the post Second World War period. James Idwal Jones was the Labour MP for Wrexham.

T W Jones chose as his lecture subject one of the great 19th Century characters of Rhosllanerchrugog, a charismatic Independent preacher. The lecturer himself belonged to a most interesting religious denomination, the Scotch Baptists, and he and his brother were regarded as leaders in the Denbighshire area. The late Dr Tom Davies of Bebington, who died in 1999, originally belonged to the same denomination, and a tribute was paid to him by Arwel Jones of Blaenau Ffestiniog, who is an acknowledged preacher in the denomination today. T W Jones also could write strict metre poetry and a few of his *"englynion"* such as his "englyn" to the Lord's Supper, will live for years to come. This gift has not been nurtured by the present Welsh Members of Parliament. T W Jones was not on his own, however, the Labour MP for Caernarfonshire, from 1945 to 1974, Goronwy O Roberts, was similarly gifted. An elder in the Presbyterian Church of Wales, he wrote an 'englyn' to the evening service:

> **Oedfa'r Hwyr**
> *Unwaith yn sŵn emynau — mi welais*
> *Am eiliad yn llathru*
> *Y groes, a dagrau Iesu,*
> *A fflach o'r gyfrinach fry*

> *Once in the atmosphere of hymn singing — I saw,*
> *in a moment the cross and the tears of Jesus,*
> *as well as a flash of the heavenly secret*

translates the insights of the Christian Socialist, Goronwy O Roberts.

Richard Huws returns to the University of Liverpool

Richard Huws was a talented sculptor and a lecturer in the Department of Architecture at the University of Liverpool. He was born in Pen-sarn Anglesey, in 1902 where his father Thomas Hughes was headmaster and then he moved to Llangoed. Richard showed aptitude to create at an early age and he was given an apprenticeship at the John Laid Birkenhead shipyard. From there he won a scholarship to the University of Liverpool to study maritime architecture and began to show a distinct talent for cartoons. He developed that talent in the 1930s and his cartoons of the Welsh literary figures, D J Williams, J Saunders Lewis and T Rowland Hughes are extremely memorable.

In 1927 he graduated and then he went to the continent, spending four years in an art school in Vienna before returning to London where he met another artist, Edrica Tyrwhitt. They married and had five children; their daughter Catherine Nagashima from Japan led the large group of exiles (over three hundred) at the National Eisteddfod of Wales held at Llanbedrgoch, Anglesey, in August 1999. Richard Huws is also remembered as the designer of the simple logo for the Welsh Nationalist Party badge, the green triangle.

During the Second World War he worked for a while at the Birkenhead shipyard, and when the company Saunders Roe moved from Merseyside to Beaumaris he went with them as his family now lived at Talwrn on the island of Anglesey. By 1953 he and his family had moved to Llanrwst. In 1955 he accepted a position in the Architecture Department of the University of Liverpool where he stayed until his retirement.

I well remember meeting Huws on a number of occasions in the early 1970s in Abercromby Square. Without a doubt he was one of the great characters of the University of Liverpool. It was said of him that as a lecturer, *"...he shows a gift to think on subjects in a very original manner"*, and he designed water machines for the Festival of Britain (1951), for the city of Tokyo (1962), for the city of Liverpool (1967). Then in 1973 he designed a water machine for Grimsby. It was placed near the Exchange Flags in Liverpool. It is sad that not one of these machines is still working.

He returned to Talwrn for his retirement and it was there that he died in February 1980. Since then the local island council has provided a plaque in memory of the accomplished sculptor, cartoonist and designer and a section of the Art Exhibition Centre at the National Eisteddfod of Wales at Anglesey in 1999 was used to exhibit some of his work.

The death of a distinguished Moderator of the Church

The Reverend Howel Harris Hughes was an outstanding minister with the Presbyterian Church of Wales on Merseyside for thirty-five years. He was a native of Anglesey and the son of the minister of Bryn-teg, Llanfair Mathafarn Eithaf, Reverend J Richard Hughes and his wife Jane, and a descendant of Nathan Hughes, an early biographer of the 18th Century Welsh Revivalist, Howell Harris of Drevecka (see *Hanes Byr o Fywyd Howel Harris*, 1838) received an excellent education and graduated with a BA (London) from University of Wales, Bangor. He was one of the first two ministerial students to receive of the University the Wales BD. Ordained in the Association at Oswestry in 1901, and he came from Caernarfon in 1909 to be minister of Princes Road Chapel, Liverpool. Hughes stayed for eighteen years and moved to Aberystwyth on his appointment as Principal of the United Theological College. He stayed in that capacity for twelve years. Then he moved back to the Liverpool area on accepting responsibility for the pastoral care for the Welsh Chapel Penuel, Portland Street, Southport and in 1939 moved to 19 Scarsbrick New Road with his wife Margaret Ellen (they were married in 1912 and had three sons). During his ministry in Southport in Liverpool (1939-1950) he was given the most prestigious positions of his denomination, Moderator of the General Assembly (1939-1941) and Moderator of the North Wales Association (1943-1944). During his period at Princes Road, whilst living at 8 Bentley Road, he wrote a commentary on the Old Testament prophet Amos, for adults attending Sunday School. It is one of the best of the commentary series, *Esboniad ar lyfr* Amos, (Caernarfon 1924) which is still useful today.

The Reverend HH Hughes died in Liverpool after a long illness on 23 November 1956 and was buried at Anfield Cemetery. An endearing gracious, humble leader, he was highly regarded on Merseyside, and reminds us very much at the end of the 20th Century of the late Cardinal Basil Hume.

A Welshman as Head of the CID in Liverpo

Great joy was expressed in so many circles in 1956 at the appointment of W Hywel Davies as Head of the CID in Liverpool. He came to Liverpool in 1932, from Betws, near Ammanford, the birthplace of the Labour politician

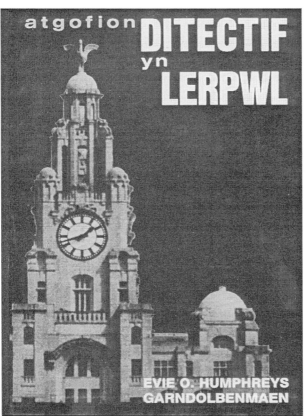

■ *Evie O Humphreys, who spent a period as a detective in Liverpool has written his autobiography*

James Griffiths, former MP for Llanelli. His wife, Agnes Mary, was from the same valley; she was born in Ammanford but their children Trevor, Glenys and Rhys were born and

brought up in Liverpool. Mrs Agnes Davies died in 1997, but W Hywel Davies still lives at the family home in Allerton.

He is a Welshman through and through, speaks Welsh as it should be spoken, and his interests in Welsh language radio and television programmes are evident. As a former rugby union player himself, he enjoys watching the major Welsh clubs like Llanelli, Swansea, Cardiff and Newport on television. W Hywel Davies has been a valuable member of Welsh chapels, namely Douglas Road Welsh Presbyterian Chapel, and, since 1974, Bethel Chapel, Heathfield Road, Liverpool. He has provided the churches with fine chrysan-themums which he has grown in his own superb garden. He retired from the world of detecting crime and has no intention of publishing his autobiography in Welsh or English though it would be well worth reading.

A call by T I Ellis to the Liverpool Welsh to tour Wales

On Friday, 1 February 1957 under the auspices of the Welsh National Society in Liverpool an excellent lecture was given by a knowledgeable member of the *"Round Britain Quiz"* team, Thomas Iorwerth Ellis (1899-1970) of Aberystwyth. He was only eight months old when his father, Tom E Ellis, the Liberal MP for Merionethshire died, and the whole responsibility rested on his mother, Annie (née Davies) from the Cwrt-mawr family in Llangeitho, Cardiganshire. The title of his lecture was *"Touring Wales"* and no-one has ever been more intimately acquainted with the land than he was. He toured Wales on foot, on his bicycle, and in his car, and by the time he came to Liverpool in 1957 his books on touring some of the counties of Wales had already been published, in particular **Crwydro Ceredigion**, *(Touring Cardiganshire)* in 1952 and **Crwydro Meirionnydd**, *(Touring Merionethshire)* in 1954. Subsequently other volumes appeared; **Crwydro Maldwyn**, *(Touring Montgomeryshire)* in 1957, **Crwydro Mynwy**, *(Touring Monmouthshire)* in 1958, **Crwydro Sir y Fflint**, *(Touring Flintshire)* in 1959 and **Crwydro Llundain**,

(Touring London) in 1971. It is a pity that he was not invited to write a book on Liverpool because he had plenty of contacts, and his daughter Meg Ellis still comes to lecture to the Welsh National Society meetings at the Bluecoat Chambers.

Dr T I Ellis was thanked most warmly by Reverend I Cyril John and Reverend J D Williams Richards, two Welsh Nonconformist ministers who knew

■ *Crwydro Meirionnydd (Touring Meirionethshire)*

Wales well. The lecturer had urged his large audience to tour Wales as often as they could, so that they could feel pride in their inheritance, a call that did not fall on deaf ears as far as the Liverpool Welsh were concerned.

St David's Day Celebrations in St Helens

The St Helens and District Welsh Society held its St David's Day celebrations in the English Congregationalist Chapel Schoolroom

■ *Welsh Chapel of St Helens Junction*

in Ormskirk Street on Saturday, 1 March 1958. The President was one of the most hardworking individuals within the Wigan Welsh Community, John R Jones. He had been elected an elder of the Welsh Calvinistic Methodist Chapel in Wigan in 1922 and

■ *Welsh Chapel of Sutton Oak*

had served as Treasurer of the Church. The guest speaker as the Reverend Gwynfryn Evans, minister of the Welsh Chapel at Chapel Road, Garston. He praised the Welsh people in exile for their loyalty and their enthusiasm. Before him there was a grand sight of two hundred and fifty Welsh people from St Helens and the towns and villages surrounding it. The arrangements were i the hands of T O Williams a native of Holyhead, and one of the leaders of the Welsh Chapel of Sutton Oak. The Secretaries were G Ellis and Lilly Barker Jones, who belonged all her life to the Welsh Chapel at Peckers Hall Road, St Helens Junction. Richie Thomas the well-known tenor from Penmachno, and hi party entertained the large gathering. He was a great attraction in the 1950s all over Wales and in the Welsh societies on Merseyside.

A harp and a choir in the Preaching Festival at Huyton Quarry

On Saturday and Sunday, 26 and 27 April 1958 the Welsh Presbyterian Chapel of Wood Lane, Huyton Quarry prepared a religious and cultural feast for the local Welsh people in the annual Preaching Festival. They invited the Reverend J D Jones from Llangaffo in Anglesey as the guest preacher. During the Saturday night meeting Telynores Llanerch, a harpist from Rhosllanerchrugog, delighted the congregation and there were evangelical songs from the Mason Choir of Wigan. The Sunday afternoon service was presided over by Samuel Williams of Johnstown near Wrexham. He was a well-known individual and a local magistrate.

The Welsh Presbyterian Chapel of Brook Street, Whiston united in the meetings and it was good to see elders of both churches together, namely Emlyn Evans, Hugh Pritchard and Hubert Jones. I remember Hubert Jones well; he was a most sincere person, who lived at Dovecot. Moses Roberts and his wife, Corwena Roberts, both elders at Brook Street, Robert Marsden and John Hughes, an original lay preachers, were all present. John Hughes used to 'phone me every Saturday morning in the early 1970s, from 'Jacob's Well'. In fact, it dawned on me, it was a laundrette in Huyton. Mrs Catherine Jones, the first woman ever to be elected an elder in the Liverpool Presbytery, was also present. She was elected in 1928 along with Thomas Jones, of 16 Warrington Road, Prescot. The organist for the festival (four services) was Mrs A Lloyd of Prion Cottages, Wood Lane, Huyton Quarry. Mrs Lloyd lost her husband, Hugh, a few weeks before the meeting. Hugh Lloyd was a collier and moved to Huyton Quarry at the end of the First World War from Ffynongroew in Flintshire to work in the mining industry in the Lancashire coalfield. He was buried at Pen Rhewl Cemetery, Mostyn.

Home of Welsh Culture

Generations of Welsh children on Merseyside were nurtured to take a delight in the Welsh language and literature although they had not received a day's formal education in the subjects. They became versed in poetry as well as Eisteddfodau, and every opportunity was taken to endow them with the Welsh literary heritage. It was part of their birthright

The sudden passing of Kate Roberts's brother in Bootle

The novelist Dr Kate Roberts mentions in a letter to her fellow literary friend J Saunders Lewis the sudden passing of her brother, John Evan Roberts, on 1 August 1959. She had gone to the Plaid Cymru's Summer School at Llangefni (31 July-4 August) and during dinner on Saturday she was called out.

■ *Kate Roberts*

"A message had come to the police station in Llangefni to say that her brother had died that morning in Liverpool. He used to suffer greatly every winter from bronchitis, but that was not the reason for his death, but thrombosis."

She had received a letter from him three days before the Summer School stating that they could not spend a fortnight's holiday in a friend's house at Abergynolwyn. She refers to her shock at her brother's death. Kate Roberts was unable to sleep at night because of her bereavement and then the skin of her face gave her trouble so that she was kept awake for at least a week.

The widow, Mrs Margaret Roberts, lived on until 19 April 1984, reaching the grand age of ninety-nine. She left two daughters, Miss Erian Roberts, of Bootle, a fount of information on the Bootle Welsh, and the late Mrs Peggy Jones of Aughton whose husband, John Bryn Jones, and daughter, Miss Elin Bryn Jones were among the mourners. It was a privilege to officiate at the thanksgiving service for that remarkable individual, Mrs Margaret Roberts of Bootle.

■ *The most concise introduction to the work of Kate Roberts in English. Published in 1974*

No Trams to Lime Street

Many of the plays written by Alun Owen are set in Liverpool, the city where he was born in 1925 to Welsh-speaking parents. Two of his plays brought him great acclaim. I refer to **No Trams to Lime Street** (1959) and

Lime Street Station

Lena, oh my Lena (1960). In 1960 he was voted by television producers the best television 'playwright'. He was criticised by some reviewers for his use of the Liverpool accent. Owen replied to them in an article in the evening paper, *Liverpool Echo:*

"I was told the accent was ridiculous, comical, absurd and very ugly. But I believe it is a lovely accent. People get married, live and die using the Liverpool accent, so I see no reason why they should not make love in the Liverpool accent."

Alun Owen wrote the film script for *A Hard Day's Night* in 1964, another success for him as it portrayed *'the fab four'.* The Beatles were fans of Alun Owen. His death, in Cardiff in 1995, was a great loss. He had been a prolific writer for radio, television and the theatre.

■ *The original Eleanor Rigby at the cemetery of Woolton parish church*

■ *The Welsh vicar, Rev J Pryce Jones, at Woolton Parish Church during the Beatles era*

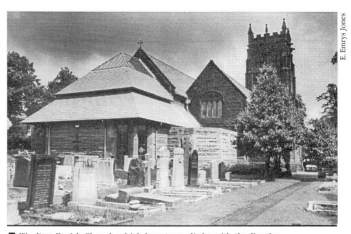

■ *Woolton Parish Church which has strong links with the Beatles*

Liverpool Cymric in great voice

■ *Liverpool Welsh Choral Union*

right mixture of likeness and contrast for such an occasion. The accompanists were Philip Brayshaw and Caleb Jarvis, who both did so much for Liverpool.

The Liverpool Cymric Vocal Union gave their sixty-fifth annual concert in the Central Hall, Liverpool on 15 April 1961, and their performance was highly praised by the music critics. In T Rowland Hughes's Welsh hymn *"Tydi a Roddaist" ("Thou givest")*, set to the music of Arwel Hughes, the conductor, Leslie Thomas, drew a finely sustained rendering and a well-managed climax, and the lightness and delicacy of the serenade from Bizet's *"Fair Maid of Perth"*, were neatly realized.

Guest stars Gita de la Guente (soprano) and Kenneth Bowen (tenor) of Llanelli and London, both in brilliant form that evening, knew just the

Cymric suffered a great loss on 22 May 1961 on the sudden death of Thomas Alun Garner (1900–1961) who had been Treasurer of the choir for twenty-five years. Deep sympathy was expressed to his wife, Mrs Gwen Garner of Cleveley Road, Allerton in her sorrow, for both had been brought up in the Welsh community of Fitzclarence Street Welsh Chapel.

■ *Liverpool Welsh Choir*

The obituary of a remarkable Liverpool Welsh missionary

Edward Hugh Williams served as a missionary in North East India for fifty-five years. He was born at 25 Premier Street, Everton, Liverpool on 22 September 1865, the son of Owen Williams (1834-1908) and Eleanor (1834-1907), both natives of Anglesey. He was baptised by Reverend Dr John Hughes in the new chapel of the Fitzclarence Welsh Calvinistic Methodists, and educated at St Saviour School, Downing Street, Everton until he was thirteen years of age. Then he was given a job in the office of John Thomas *"stock and share broker"* in Sweeting Street. Afterwards he worked at Dodd and Oulton office, and then for his uncles, Thomas Brothers, of Hornby Street, before being given a job at the Sun Foundry of Smith's in Dale Street. E H Williams was moved to their head office in Glasgow, and he became active in the United Presbyterian Church, Renfield Street. It was there that he heard the Reverend James Gray of Rafpuntania, India pleading for missionaries. His appeal was:

"Isn't there here a young man who is willing to offer himself to go out to India for the love of Christ?"
He did not respond to the appeal immediately, but within a month, in his lodgings in Parson Street, he expressed his feelings to the minister of the

church, Reverend James Grierson Scott, and began receiving tuition in Latin at the manse. In February 1885 he moved back to Liverpool (10 Conyers Street, Kirkdale) and in the evenings he attended Latin and Greek courses at the YMCA in Mount Pleasant. He was also given opportunities by the various societies in Fitzclarence Street to speak in public. Edward Williams was accepted to the Theological College in Bala in 1891, and then went for a few months for medical training at Glasgow. He was ordained before leaving for India on the *"City of Corinth"* on 23 September 1893 and arrived with his wife on October 26th. His wife, Edith Ann (née Roberts), was from Ruthin and had for a time been a member of Fitzclarence Street chapel. They were met in Calcutta by George Sykes of Sykes & Company of Great Lane, who operated on behalf of the Liverpool office of the mission. By 31 October they were in Chatak where they were welcomed by J Pengwern Jones. Edward Williams and the medical missionary Dr Edward Williams were at the missionary station of Stella. Edward and his wife travelled to the villages of Laitkynsew, Tynger, Lyngkom and Synnei and over the years the work increased. Mrs Williams died in 1905. Both had witnessed the Religious Revival on the hills of Khasia and Jaintia. Edward Williams had tremendous sympathy with the ethos of the Keswick Movement, and he brought the spirit of that movement to the lives of the villagers of Laitkynsew, Mawphlang, Rangthong and Mawiang. They prayed for the Revival.

After the Revival Williams was in Mawphlang and Jowai and from 1910 looked after the Shangpung District. He was an outstanding pioneer, the first missionary to pioneer in the inaccessible region of Lyngnagam. It was a real struggle to arrive there to minister as there were difficulties all the way, but he was not a man to flinch from the task at hand. He had no fear of man or beast, and worked diligently among the Mikir tribe. They were very primitive people but renowned for their kindness. One of the most horrifying weaknesses among the inhabitants of the village of the Mikir tribe was their habit of eating opium.

He travelled to the valleys of the Mikir people. They built their villages in the middle of the forests, but the missionary succeeded in persuading them to evangelize. He baptised the children, accepted those of every age, young, middle-age and old, who were ready to become church members and he preached the comforts of the Gospel in the chapels and in the open air with the assistance of an interpreter from the Mikir. He also made sure that native teachers were sent to the villages.

E H Williams travelled a number of these journeys in an interesting way on the pages of the **Cenhadwr** *(The Missionary)*. He was a country doctor in the true sense of the word as well, and G Angell Jones has described in the **Cenhadwr** this part of his missionary life and how a large number of babies in Khasia and Jaintia, *"slipped easily into the world through his ministry and his black bag."* He married Gertrude Mary Williams, his second wife, and a number of children were born to them. She died in 1929. Then in 1936 he married the missionary Annie Dorothy (Nancy) Williams, and a son and a daughter were born to them. Their daughter, from this third marriage, Bethan Williams, was one of the last Welsh Presbyterians to leave for the mission field, which she did in 1966.

E H Williams and Mrs Nancy Williams returned to Wales in 1947. They had completed a remarkable ministry, had cared in turn for every district on the Khasia and Jaintia Hills, had undertaken all kinds of responsibilities and endeared themselves to generations of people in India. They lived at Ravenhill, Swansea and he died on 30 September 1962.

The death of a retired company director

Suddenly on 30 October 1963 at the Royal Alexandra Hospital Rhyl, Annie Margaret Jones devoted, eldest daughter of the late Mr and Mrs J T Jones of Everton, died at the age of sixty-three. Her father, John T Jones, had been in business for thirty years as a draper and funeral director in Breck Road, Everton. He died in 1937. Mrs Annie Jones, his wife and the mother of Annie Margaret, lived in Abergele during the Second World War, but she returned to Liverpool and attended Heathfield Road Welsh Presbyterian Church for fifteen years. She returned to Abergele where she died in her ninetieth year.

Miss Annie Margaret Jones had been a company director for over forty years connected with Somerville & Company Ltd, general produce merchants, of North John Street, Liverpool. She had been a Sunday School Superintendent and Band of Hope leader and had held many other positions at Fitzclarence Welsh Chapel where her father was an elder for twenty-five years. Miss Jones retired to Ael-y-Bryn, Clifton Rise, Abergele and left £6,774 gross, £6,644 net. Her mother survived her in great sorrow.

Herbert Hughes

Heathfield Road Presbyterian Church of Wales as it was during the period when Mrs Annie Jones was a member at the chapel in Smithdown Place (near Penny Lane)

Fifty years with a city firm: Myfanwy Owen

Miss Myfanwy Owen, the daughter of Mr and Mrs Robert Owen of Caerllechau in Dwyran, Anglesey, became a key figure in the Liverpool Welsh Community. She went to the Liverpool offices of Owen Owen Ltd straight from Llangefni County School, and spent her whole working life with the company serving under seven company secretaries.

She retired in 1964 after fifty years with Owen Owen Ltd and received many gifts from her wide circle of friends at the party given by the directors to mark her loyal and dedicated service. She lived at 36 Green Lane, Mossley Hill, and was a very loyal and generous member of Heathfield Road Presbyterian Church of Wales. After retirement she decided to stay in Liverpool because she liked the activities of the Liverpool Welsh Community and would regularly visit her sisters and other relatives in the Dwyran area.

I knew her well and have very fond memories of the welcome given by Miss Myfanwy Owen and travelled back from my holiday to conduct her funeral service in Dwyran where she died on 21 August 1973.

■ *Owen Owen store and office during the period of Miss Myfanwy Owen*

First volume of the Wavertree Welsh poet

In 1965 the first volume of the poetry of R J Roberts of Deepfield Road, Wavertree, Liverpool appeared under the title **Clychau'r Gynghanedd**, *(The Bells of the Gynghanedd)* published by Gee Press of Denbigh. R J Roberts had the same gift as William Edwards (Gwilym Deudraeth) of being able to write "englynion" in the English language. In his volume he presents some of these "englynion", two of them concerning one of his great delights, football:

■ *RJ Roberts*

The Goalie
Hail the goalie, mighty man, - in his team
Finest type of guardian;
Check their tricks and kicks he can,
Hardy, steady custodian.

The Final
Stalwarts who play so stylish, - win a goal,
Then a game of polish
Dies away, do as you wish,
It's a final, let's finish.

Naval Advert
Wanted young men of twenty –
with a will,
See the world, it's easy;
Turn over to our navy,
Get a suit and go to sea.

And then he descries the individual who destroys fellowship under the title,

The Tale Carrier:
A low sort and sly is he, - wary too,
For a tale to carry;
Bosses who find him busy
Amply use this employee.

And finally, on The Modern Miss of the 1960s:
A young man's real fancy – draws a smile,
Dresses smart and pretty;
A bit of modern beauty,
In short, a smasher is she.

■ *His handwriting*

Arthur Rowland a Garston bank manager, retires

The Bont, the quarterly publication of the Rotary Movement in North Wales, Wirral and Merseyside, which has been edited since 1997 by myself

Governor of 1180 of the Rotary area (which covers Mid and North Wales and adjacent parts of England from Oswestry to Chester, Wirral and Merseyside). In 1960 he travelled to the USA to be trained as a District Governor. His year of office would then be 1960-1961. He also served as Chairman of the Garston Federation of Trade and was a member of the local branch of the Liverpool Personal Service Society.

Married with two sons and a daughter, Arthur Rowland delighted in his family. He was also very conscious of the need to assist charitable movements in the local community.

Arthur Rowland, of Menlove Avenue, Calderstones, served for forty-five years in the banking world and for twenty years was the manager of the National Westminster Bank in Garston. Before moving to Garston he had served in the Manchester area, at the London head office, and at Burton-on-Trent. Proud of his Welsh background, Arthur Rowland was a very prominent Rotarian. Belonging to the Rotary Club of Garston he became District

Rotary in Brief

Life and work of Enid Wyn Jones

Enid Wyn Jones

This remarkable philanthropist was born in Wrexham on 17 January 1909, the only daughter of Dr David Llewelyn Williams (1870-1947) and his wife (née Price) of Rhyl. The family moved to Cardiff in 1912 and Enid was educated at the Welsh Girls' School between 1919 and 1926 in Ashford, Kent from where she proceeded to the Domestic Science College in Cardiff (1926-1927). She then trained as a nurse at Cardiff Royal Infirmary. She met her future husband, the physician Dr Emyr Wyn Jones (1909-1999), on the first sea journey of the Welsh League of Youth in August 1933, and they were married on 9 September 1936 in Liverpool. They had a

daughter, Carys (who recently retired from the University of Liverpool) and a son, Professor Richard Gareth Jones of the University of Wales, Bangor.

Their home at 15 Sandringham Drive, Liverpool was rendered uninhabitable in 1941 as the result of the massive bombing attacks of the Second World War. As a mother, Enid had to make a secure place for the children at the homestead of Llety'r Eos, Llansannan, Denbighshire, but she continued to visit regularly her second home at 28 Rodney Street, Liverpool.

An ecumenical at heart, Enid Wyn Jones belonged to the Presbyterian Church of Wales, as well as the Society of Friends. At a time when women preachers were rare she gave substantial service for years to the Welsh-speaking congregations in South Lancashire, especially the chapels in the St Helens district. Her melodious singing voice and her ability as a pianist were additional assets. She was a fluent speaker who prepared her addresses with meticulous care.

After several years of practical social

welfare in the inner-city and dockland areas of Liverpool, under the aegis of the YWCA and the Free Churches, Enid Wyn Jones was drawn into the wider fields of service. Her commitment to the women's work of the Merseyside Free Church Federal Council was evident, and during 1958-1959 she was President of the National Free Church Federal Women's Council, being only the second Welsh woman to attain that honour. She became President of the Welsh Council of the YWCA, Vice-President of the Council for England and Wales (1959-1967) and a member of the World Council of the YWCA, in which capacity she attended world conferences. Towards the end of the quadrennial World Council at Melbourne, Australia in 1967 she sustained, without any warning, a subarachnoid haemorrhage. After a measure of recovery, and accompanied by her husband, she had a fatal recurrence over Bangkok on the flight home on 15 September 1967. She was buried at the Henry Rees

E. Emrys Jones

■ *The Rodney Street home*

Memorial Chapel cemetery, Llansannan, on September 20th. Many of the articles which she contributed to the ***Free Church Chronicle*** and the Welsh language press describing her travels were included in the books published after her death and edited by her husband, namely the bilingual volume ***In memory of Enid Wyn Jones***, published by her husband privately in 1968), and the Welsh language volume, published by Modern Welsh Publications Ltd, Liverpool, under the title ***Cyfaredd Cof,*** *(A Beautiful Memory)* which appeared in 1970. My wife, Mrs Meinwen Rees, did a great deal of work preparing the English articles and translating them into Welsh for the ***Cyfaredd Cof*** publication. The article and address delivered at the Free Church Conference at Folkestone in March 1958 that sum up her life of service is entitled, *"****A Housewife in Search of God****"* and was published by the Free Church Council as a pamphlet.

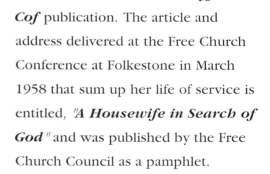

A portrait of the Reverend Owen Prys Davies of Childwall

Owen Prys Davies hailed from Llandecwyn, in Merionethshire and was born in 1914. After school and college he became a minister with the Welsh (Wesleyan) Methodist Church and served a number of circuits. But his stay in Liverpool was longer than any of the others. It was at Llansilin, in Montgomeryshire that he met his future wife, Mary, a supportive individual and a true homemaker. They had two daughters, Marian Prys Davies (of Childwall) and Gwyddfid Davies (who lives in Bangor).

It was O Prys Davies who saw the opportunity with the renovation of the Central Hall in Renshaw Street to centralize the Welsh chapels of Trinity Road, Bootle, Spellow Lane, Oakfield in Anfield; Mynydd Seion (Princes Road) and Garston into a new cause in the heart of Liverpool. He possessed a strong voice, plenty of humour and an endearing personality. Reverend O Prys Davies passed into glory at Broadgreen Hospital on 6 May 1995 at the age of ninety-one and the service for the family was held at

■ *Reverend O Prys Davies*

Springwood Crematorium on May 11th. His minister, Reverend E Gwyn Hughes paid him the tribute which was published in the Welsh language community newspaper for Merseyside and Manchester, *Angor* (July 1995) page 1.

A portrait of the Reverend John David Williams Richards of Childwall

A prominent minister with the Free Churches in Liverpool, John David Williams Richards was born at Ystalyfera in the Swansea Valley, though he had deep roots in Ffaldybrenin, Carmarthenshire. Ordained in 1935 after completing his theological training at Brecon Memorial College, he ministered at Pontycymer and Clydach before moving as minister to the Welsh Congregationalist Chapel, Belmont Road, Liverpool, in 1945. He continued to minister after they moved from Belmont Road to Woolton Road, and was also pastor of Salem, Hawthorne Road, Bootle.

■ *The site where the Chapel used to be in Belmont Road*

J D Williams Richards took a great interest in the Free Churches. He became the Secretary of the Merseyside Free Church Federal Council, and served effectively for decades. He supervised the transfer of the Free Church Centre from Lord Street to Tarleton Street and took great delight in the Welsh Books Section of its library.

He served day after day at the Book Centre until 1981. He was influential in his own denomination, became Chairman of the Council (and arguably should have been made President) and was Secretary of the local Liverpool and District Connexion from 1951 until 1992. His wife hailed from Llanerch-y-medd, Anglesey and they had two daughters.

■ *Reverend R J Pritchard who ministered at Belmont Road*

■ *Reverend Eurof Walters, a distinguished minister at Belmont Road*

■ *Deacons of Belmont Road with the Reverend JD Williams Richards*

Walton Prison Welsh Chaplaincy

◀ *Leaders of Walton Park Welsh Chapel in the 1930's, a chapel that gave sterling care to the Welsh-speaking prisoners of Walton Prison*

In 1970 the Reverend Williams Jones, Minister of Stanley Road Presbyterian Church of Wales, was appointed by the Home Office as part-time Welsh Chaplain to Walton Prison in Liverpool. He received full support from his own Presbytery and also from the Ministry of Healing of his denomination and its centre at Caernarfon. They gave him financial help at times. For example, a tape recorder was provided to assist him in the preparation of Welsh religious services. His denomination's Ministry of Healing held Reverend William Jones in high regard. After all, during his theological training he became friends with three other students, and they all became extremely conscientious within the Healing Ministry when they themselves became ministers. The four were J Glyn Williams, of Aberdovey; M Meirion Roberts, of Llandudno; W Bryn Roberts, a product of the Welsh life of Blackburn; and William Jones himself, a native of Groes, a village outside Denbigh. William Jones remained as Chaplain at Walton until he retired, due to ill health, in 1978. It was a fruitful ministry for which he was highly regarded by the inmates as well as the prison staff.

Electing Presbyterian leaders

In 1971 four Welsh Presbyterian chapels elected seven elders to serve four congregations. Heathfield Road Presbyterian Church of Wales elected Dr R Arthur Hughes and Mr Vincent Roberts. Dr Hughes had served as a medical missionary in North East India and had already been an elder for twenty-four years in Shillong. Mr Roberts of Ramilies Road, had given a great deal of his time to supporting the children and youth of the church and was a practical person. At Edge Lane Welsh Chapel, Miss Nina C Hughes of Newsham Park was chosen, while at

■ *Dr R Arthur Hughes (1910-1996) as Moderator of the Presbyterian Church of Wales*

Eglwys y Drindod, Princes Road, Miss Mary B Owen, a teacher, and Mrs Mair Oswy Davies, the widow of the Minister Reverend Ifor Oswy Davies, were elected. The Welsh chapel at Rake Lane elected Mrs Marian Owen, a native of Abersoch in the Llŷn peninsula, and Mr W R Byrne to be the leaders of the Welsh Presbyterian community in Wallasey and New Brighton. The election of these leaders was carried out under the stewardship of two statesmen of the Presbytery, Reverend W D Jones and Reverend E Watkin Jones.

■ *Reverend E Watkin Jones, Minister at Heathfiels Road Welsh Chapel from 1949 until 1967*

The closure of Whiston Welsh Chapel

The last service held at Whiston Welsh Presbyterian Chapel was conducted on Sunday afternoon, 19 December 1972 with His Honour Judge John Edward Jones presiding as Moderator of the Liverpool Presbytery. The congregation at Whiston, Prescot had decided to join the Welsh Chapel at Huyton Quarry. At the last service an address was given by Mr Evan Roberts who had been an elder at Blackburn Welsh Chapel and a zealous supporter of all those Welsh chapels in the St Helens district. He had been born and brought up in Blackburn and had a natural empathy with those who had been faithful at Whiston. Other stalwarts at Whiston were Mrs Corwena Roberts, of Dragon's Lane, and Mrs Catherine Jones, one of the earliest female elders among the Welsh Presbyterians. She was elected in 1928 when she lived at 92 South Avenue, Prescot. I remember her well and I was present at the Liverpool Presbytery in 1968 when she was congratulated on completing forty years as an elder at Whiston. She had known the stalwart of the cause, Moses Roberts of Sinclair Avenue, Prescot.

Long ministry and a friend of Whiston Chapel

Reverend Richard Aethwy Jones (1867-1941), who spent 43 years at Newsham Park Welsh Presbyterian Chapel, has the record of the 'longest single pastorate' in the whole history of the Liverpool Welsh Churches. He often preached at Whiston Welsh Presbyterian Chapel.

An outstanding lecture by Owen Owen

At a meeting of the Liverpool Presbytery of the Presbyterian Church of Wales at 23 Temple Street, on Wednesday 12 September 1973, an outstanding lecture was delivered by Mr Owen Owen, MA, of Garston, on the 18th Century Welsh Calvinistic Methodist revivalist, Howell Harris (1714-1773) of Trefeca near Talgarth in Breconshire. His greatest contribution to the life of the Welsh nation was his preaching and he has been called one of the makers of modern Wales.

It was obvious to us all that Mr Owen Owen had done a great deal of research for his lecture. A native of Caernarfonshire, he became a teacher and headmaster in Liverpool. I remember how he was revered as Headmaster of Northway Primary School. He was fluent in both Welsh and English and an articulate lecturer. In 1937, while he lived at *"Ingledene"*, Aigburth Road, Owen Owen was elected an elder of Garston Welsh Presbyterian Chapel and he served for years as its Secretary. I only wished that I had a tape recorder with me on the night I heard Owen Owen remembering the powerful ministry of Howell Harris.

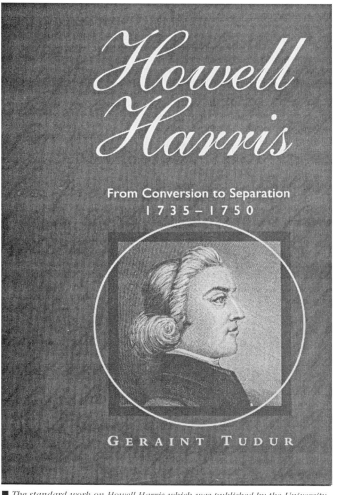

Howell Harris

From Conversion to Separation
1 7 3 5 – 1 7 5 0

GERAINT TUDUR

■ *The standard work on Howell Harris which was published by the University of Wales Press in 2000*

A tribute to Dan Thomas

A banker by profession, Dan Thomas was a warm-hearted individual who had great concerns. Born in Llanerchymedd, Anglesey in 1889, he started working at Martins Bank as a young lad of sixteen. He came under the influence of the bank manager, George M Ll Davies, the Liverpool Welshman who eventually became a pacifist. It was Davies who persuaded him to join the Royal Welsh Fusiliers in 1911. Within a few months Davies had seen how obscene war was, a form of slavery, and he left, but Dan Thomas stayed. He was made captain, wounded in France in 1916, and then went back to Wrexham as a recruiting officer. Among the conscientious objectors on whom he served warrants was George M Ll Davies. Indeed Davies stayed with him the night before he was placed under arrest!

After returning to the head office of Martins Bank in Liverpool he led a campaign to form a trade union, the Bank Officers Guild. He was later its President for four years. In Liverpool he played an active part in the Labour Party being Secretary of the Granby Ward, but before he left for Cardiff in

1937, he joined the Welsh Nationalist Party like the rest of his family, and in

■ *Dan Thomas*

particular his son Dewi-Prys Thomas and daughter Rhiannon Evans. He fought the parliamentary seat of Wrexham in 1959 for Plaid Cymru and served as the Treasurer of the Party (1950-1970). He died at Porthmadog in 1974.

Fifty years as a Minister of Religion

In 1975 the Reverend Robert Emrys Evans, of Birkenhead, was congratulated on completing fifty years in the

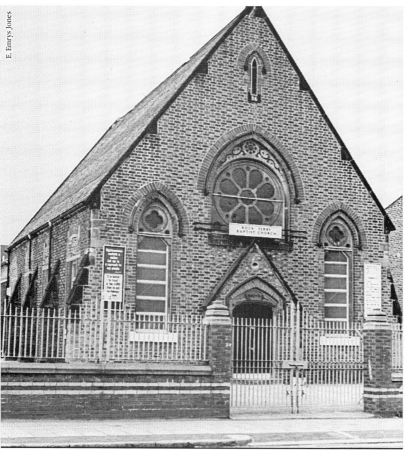

E. Emrys Jones

■ *Rock Ferry Welsh Chapel*

ministry of the Presbyterian Church of Wales, forty-six of them spent on Merseyside. He remained a student throughout the years and read extensively in theology. He was, like most able scholars, rather unconcerned with ambition and being showered

with honours by his denomination. He much preferred study, including reading the The Expository Times, to being published. He wrote very little, an occasional piece for Welsh periodicals, and edited the Liverpool Welsh monthly magazine, **Y Glannau**, *(The Shore)*.

Emrys Evans ministered at West Kirby, then Rock Ferry and Ellesmere Port, and did a stint at the Foreign Mission offices in Falkner Street. But study remained his favoured activity, and his wife, Mrs Elizabeth Emrys Evans, was a very able teacher and scholar in her own right. Her efforts to write the history of the Birkenhead Welsh never saw the light of day but it would have been an excellent account of the Welsh presence by one taught in Bangor by the renowned Sir John Edward Lloyd.

Gosh it's Tosh

John Toshack could play football as well as write poetry. His volume of poetry *Gosh it's Tosh* was published in 1976 by Duckworth & Co Ltd of London. His poem *"A Goalden Night"* is a masterpiece for all Liverpool football supporters:

> *"We went straight at them from the start,*
> *Their whole defence was ripped apart.*
> *Our pre-match plans went to the letter,*
> *Has any Liverpool team played better?*
>
> *Ray Clemence kicks a long high ball,*
> *And Barcelona are about to fall.*
> *For Kevin Keegan wins the race,*
> *And flicks it on into a space.*
> *By my right foot the ball is wet,*
> *And in a flash it's in the net!*
>
> *A Goalden night and what a thrill,*
> *It's Liverpool one, Barcelona nil.*
> *One away goal will suit us fine,*
> *And I'm so pleased that it was mine.*
>
> *Now all we want to do is sing,*
> *But let's remember just one thing,*
> *Midst all the fuss let's not forget,*
> *We haven't reached the final yet!"*

John Toshack joined the Reds from his local club, Cardiff for £110,000 in November 1970 and proved himself at Anfield. He won an FA Cup-winners' medal in 1974 and was largely responsible for Liverpool winning the UEFA Cup in 1972-3. In 1975-6 he excelled himself, and implemented his poetic licence by scoring the only goal in Barcelona which set Liverpool on their way to the Final. The same season John Toshack won his second championship medal, and a third the following season. After 169 league appearances for Liverpool he left in 1978 to join Swansea City as player manager. At the Vetch he was an outstanding success guiding the Welsh club from the Fourth to First Division. Toshack also took his total of Welsh caps to forty.

The skills of Kevin Ratcliffe of Everton FC

Liverpool Daily Post & Echo

■ *Kevin Ratcliffe*

Kevin Ratcliffe was the most successful captain in the entire history of Everton Football Club, ("the Toffees"). He hails from Mancot in Flintshire, the same area which has been placed on the map by the wizardry of Michael Owen of Liverpool in more recent times. Ratcliffe came to Everton as an apprentice player in 1977 and showed great aptitude and skill. Within three years he was in the first team as a full back and, though he had some difficulties, manager Howard Kendall showed enough faith in him to move him to centre half. He never flinched

from responsibility, and he was in the Welsh side that played Czechoslovakia in 1981. Altogether he represented Wales in international football fifty-eight times. Soon he was captain of Wales as well as Everton. He had a phenomenal run in which he skippered "the Toffees" to victory in two First Division Championships (1984/5 and 1986/7) and runner-up in 1985/6. Everton were FA Cup Runners-up in 1985, 1986 and 1989 and had a host of other near misses in the Milk Cup (1983/84), and Simond Cup (1988/89) and Zenith Data Systems Cup (1990/91). It was a delight for him to receive the accolade for leading Everton successfully to victory in the European Cup – Winners Cup in 1985.

Liverpool Daily Post & Echo

■ *'a phenomenal run'*

A novel on the Birkenhead Welsh

Marion Eames is a Welsh novelist and short story writer who is proud of her Merseyside connections. Born in Birkenhead, she was brought up in Dolgellau, and had a variety of positions in the world of librarianship, the political life of Plaid Cymru, as editor of the weekly **Dydd** in Dolgellau,

■ *Marion Eames*

and as a student at the Guildhall School of Music, London, before joining the BBC as a radio producer in 1959, remaining until her retirement in 1980. Her first novel, **Y Stafell Ddirgel,** *(The Mystery Room),* appeared in 1969 and others followed. To us on Merseyside her novel, **I Hela Cnau** *(To Collect Nuts)* published in 1978 had a great appeal as it depicts the coming of the Welsh during the growth of Birkenhead in the middle of the 19th Century. My youngest son, Iefin, particularly enjoyed **I Hela Cnau**. It is no wonder that Marion Griffith Williams has won three awards

from the Welsh Arts Council. Her late husband, Griffith Williams, was a talented individual in the world of journalism, while her mother and her brother Trefor Jones, a grocer in Birkenhead, were kind-hearted and lovable individuals. We saw and heard Marion Eames at the Welsh re-union on 14 October 2000 in Liverpool.

The retirement of the Reverend Robert Maurice Williams, minister at Waterloo and Southport

Reverend Robert Maurice Williams was a Presbyterian minister who spent twenty-seven years in North Liverpool and Southport. He was born in 1911 in Bethesda, Caernarfonshire. His father was very well known as a harpist and greatly admired by the poet R Williams Parry. He came to Liverpool from Cemaes, Anglesey in September 1952 as minister of the Welsh chapels of Waterloo and Southport. 'RM' as he was affectionately known, was an exceptional pastor of both churches, regularly visiting those of his members who were indisposed. An enthusiastic Welshman, he served for years as editor of the Merseyside Welsh language monthly magazine, Y Bont, (The Bridge). A gifted harpist

A tribute to Grace Ellen Roberts who did so much in Waterloo Chapel as an accompanist

like his father, he was in his student days a staunch propagandist for Plaid Cymru.

R M Williams was a poet in the strict metres, and wrote some fine *"englynion"*. A kind person, he assisted his far-flung flock in Southport by calling on those who had difficulties in reaching the chapel in Portland Street. He was ably supported at his home in Myers Road West, Crosby, by his wife, another very hospitable person. He retired in 1979 and they decided to move to the town of Llanrwst where he enjoyed his well-earned leisure in bardic circles and preaching in the chapels. He died at Glan Clwyd Hospital in January 1987.

E. Emrys Jones

Waterloo Presbyterian Church of Wales, Crosby Road South

Welsh boxer dies after title fight

Johnny Owen, the shy but brilliant Welsh bantamweight, died in Los Angeles on Tuesday, 4 November 1980 after being knocked out by the Mexican Lupe Pintor during a fierce contest for the world crown. He had been in a coma ever since the fight six weeks earlier.

The thin, almost weedy, twenty-four year old was born in Merthyr Tydfil and hardly looked like a world-class boxer. He made his professional debut at Pontypool on 30 September 1976, beating George Sutton on points over eight rounds. From then onwards he won fight after fight. In 1978 for example, he had seven professional contests and won them all. But at Los Angeles his dream turned into tragedy. As Johnny went down in the tenth round his head struck the boards with a tremendous thud and the referee stopped the fight without making the usual count. Johnny was taken

from the ring on a stretcher underwent a three-hour operation to remove a blood clot from his brain, but never recovered.

Johnny Owen had commanded enormous affection throughout Wales and among many boxing enthusiasts in the Merseyside Welsh community.

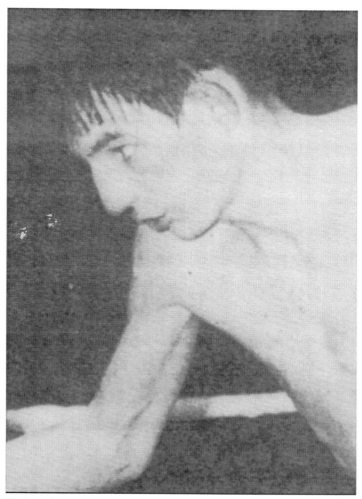

■ *Johnny Owen*

Riots hit Toxteth

The date 5 July 1981 will never be forgotten for on that day the police were forced to withdraw from Upper Parliament Street, Liverpool when they admitted that the mob had gone *"out of control"*. On July 10th youths again rampaged through the high-streets and even the side roads of the Granby Ward and Lodge Lane area of Liverpool, and those of us who worked or ministered in the area were frightened. This area had been a stronghold of the Welsh community until the 1970s and even in 1981 there were Welsh-speaking families living in the Granby Ward.

I was involved in many interviews for the media regarding the riots. One I remember well. It was done near the old Rialto, a building which had a strong Welsh connection. The architect had been D J Lewis who in 1962 became the Lord Mayor of Liverpool. A native of Aberystwyth, he served the city of Liverpool well. It was sad to see one of his creations disappearing in flames.

The riot made us all search for the root causes, thought to include unemployment, poor housing and racism. The Welsh-born Conservative politician, Michael Heseltine, came to the rescue announcing a package of measure to help depressed areas like Toxteth.

■ *Alderman D J Lewis*

The magic of Ian Rush

Ian Rush was one of the most successful Liverpool football players of the 1980s and 1990s. Born in St Asaph on 20 October 1961, he was brought up on Deeside in the town of Flint. He signed up for Liverpool in April 1980 from Chester City. He was then a quiet eighteen year old, much happier passing the ball to one of the players in the forward line than scoring himself. One day he met Bob Paisley and asked him for a pay rise. Paisley replied without hesitation that he could give him more money only if he started scoring more goals and that if he did not have a good shot he would never be able to do that. This was the beginning of a unique football career. He came into the side in place of another brilliant forward, Kenny Dalglish. It was a golden opportunity for Rush that December, but he had to wait until the following April's League Cup Final Replay to show the Liverpool supporters his potential, against West Ham. But he was still hampered because he was very much a right-footer. It is a great credit to him that he eventually mastered the game sufficiently well to score goals with both feet.

■ *Ian Rush*

One of his best early games was on 6 November 1982 in a local Derby against Everton. Liverpool had a wonderful team: Grobelaar, Neal, Kennedy, Thompson, Johnson, Hansen, Dalglish, Lee Rush, Lawrenson and

Souness. The Celts were prominent in the Liverpool side and Everton too had Celtic players in the persons of McMahon and the Welsh goalkeeper Neville Southall. But to Rush it was an unforgettable day and he scored four goals, equalling the record that had stood since Fred Howe achieved four in the Merseyside Derby of 1935. If it was not for Southall he would have scored more. The Liverpool supporters in the large crowd (52,741) were delighted with Rush.

He shared numerous honours in the eighties: The European Cup 1983/4, League Championship 1981/2, 1982/83, 1983/4, 1985/86, 1989/90, FA Cup 1985/86, 1988/89, 1991/92 and League Cup 1980/81, 1981/82, 1982/83, 1983/84, 1994/95. He found the net in more games for the League Cup and Merseyside Derbies than anyone else in the 20th Century. Rush insisted on playing for Wales, received seventy-three caps, and scored twenty-eight goals, which was a national record. Many a supporter from the Liverpool Welsh community had a tear in their eyes when Ian Rush left Anfield for Leeds in 1996. He had been a great celebrity in Liverpool.

Liverpool Daily Post & Echo

■ *Ian Rush and Joey Jones*

Very Reverend Derrick Walters, fourth Dean of the Liverpool Anglican Cathedral

Derrick Walters had grown up before the Second World War, as a Welsh Independent in the Swansea area, and Liverpool in the 1980s and 1990s owes him a great debt. He had been engaged in a varied ministry before he followed Edward Patey in Liverpool as Dean of the Anglican Cathedral in 1983. Derrick Walters had ministered at Swansea, Sheffield and Derby before moving with his wife Joan and sons David and Michael to The Close in Salisbury. It was a very interesting move from Salisbury to Liverpool, but he immediately saw the potential of the Anglican Cathedral in Liverpool and, through his efforts, it became an attraction for tourists from all over the world, including Wales. He had dynamism and it was through his efforts that the buildings around the cathedral came into existence. One would not claim that he was an

■ *The Anglican Cathedral*

inspiring preacher but he was always an inspiration to those around him. Every cathedral needs a dynamic dean if it is to succeed. Liverpool, in the post-1981 riots era, was fortunate to have the vision of the Very Reverend Derrick Walters. In his trying illness he was an example to all of courage and faith, a dedicated man of God. His death in Liverpool in 1999 silenced on earth a priest of commitment to the worshipping community and an entrepreneur who had unwavering determination to bring to fruition as many of his schemes as he could in his adopted city.

In praise of Goronwy Evan Thomas

Goronwy Evan Thomas was an orthopaedic surgeon. Born at Cyffylliog, Denbighshire on 22 March 1907, the son of Hugh and Mary Thomas, he received his education at the local primary school, County School Denbigh and the Universities of Liverpool, Edinburgh and London. He studied engineering but changed his mind and turned to medicine. He qualified in medicine in the University of Liverpool in 1932, again under the University of London, the following year, then he obtained the FRCS (Edinburgh) in 1936.

He spent his whole career in Liverpool, was consultant to the David Lewis Northern Hospital, the Royal Liverpool children's Hospital, Broadgreen Hospital and was in great demand in a number of hospitals in Clwyd. Goronwy Thomas possessed great surgical skills, was a good friend to his patients and the Welsh flocked to him. He married Morfudd (née Owen) and they had one son, Huw Owen Thomas, FRCS, who followed in his father's footsteps, in fact they worked together for a period.

Goronwy Thomas had a large number of interests, including fishing, shooting, reading and an abiding interest in the history of medicine. He delivered many lectures on the bone setters of Anglesey like Hugh Owen Thomas and his wife's nephew, Sir Robert Jones. He worked for some years with T P Murray, an expert bone setter who had been a student and devoted assistant to Sir Robert Jones. He was chosen as President of the Liverpool Medical Institution in 1969. He was keenly interested in the history of Liverpool and of Wales.

A member of Bethel Presbyterian Church of Wales, Liverpool 15, he always gave a warm welcome to his minister at home at Eastleigh, Mossley Hill Road. He was a member of numerous societies, including the Cambrian Archaeological Society and the Twenty-Five Club in Liverpool.

He had a long, distressing illness, suffered more than one seizure, and in the end lost most of his speech. Even then he did not lose his fighting spirit, and one of his colleagues after his death on 23 June 1984 said, *"and we shall not see his like again"*. The thanksgiving service was held at Bethel Heathfield Road Chapel and Emrys O Roberts gave me as the officiating member a wonderful tribute on the way out of Bethel when he said, *"a noncomformist service at its very best"*. Goronwy Thomas gave service at its very best, and as a surgeon, storyteller, generous host, real doctor and a dependable friend he had no superior.

■ *The Liverpool Medical Institution showing the original building and the new extension*

E Emrys Jones

■ *Hope University College, the meeting place for the Welsh Twenty-five Club in Liverpool*

Dewi-Prys Thomas, a talented architect

■ *Dewi-Prys Thomas*

One of Wales's foremost architects was born in Liverpool in 1916, the son of Dan and Elizabeth Thomas, and was educated at the Liverpool Institute before following a course in architecture for a degree at the University of Liverpool. He also pursued a course in town planning. Dewi-Prys Thomas won a series of prizes in architecture, and was appointed a lecturer in the subject immediately after completing his course.

He was later appointed as the first Principal of the School of Architecture of the University of Wales, Cardiff, where he became known to a generation of students as an inspired communicator. One of his extraordinary achievements as Principal was to ensure that at least 50% of every year's intake came from Wales. A number of his students, such as the entertainer and local government politician in Gwynedd Dafydd Iwan, have written on his role as an academic. Every year a lecture is given, in his memory, at the National Eisteddfod of Wales. He was one of the first from the world of architecture to prepare designs for book covers, and was responsible for the dusk jackets of the Welsh novels of T Rowland Hughes. His death in 1985 was hugely felt in the world of architecture.

Neville Southall, Everton FC

Neville Southall

Neville Southall was one of the greatest players at Everton Fooball Club in the 1980s, though he did not find it easy when he arrived from Bury. Everton paid £150,000 for him but he was soon on loan to Port Vale until Jim Arnold gave him a team place. By 1983 he was the first choice as goalkeeper and this remained the situation for the next fourteen years. He became one of the best goalkeepers in Britain, and was capped ninety-two times for Wales. In 1985 he was chosen as Footballer of the Year and he received an MBE in 1996.

Neville Southall played five hundred and seventy-eight times in the League, seventy times in games for the Cup,

thirteen times in Europe and ninety times on other occasions making a total of seven-hundred and fifty-one games between 1981 and 1998. He is six feet one inch tall and was born in the seaside resort of Llandudno in 1958. His early teams were in North Wales, namely Llandudno Swifts, Conwy United and Bangor City, which is struggling these days. Southall cannot and will not leave Llandudno; even on Saturday nights he used to travel back from the London fixtures so as to be with his family and friends. He did much to enrich the Liverpool Welsh scene in his Everton years.

Neville Southall

Companion to Welsh literature

In 1986 two volumes, one in Welsh and the other in English, were published by the University of Wales Press and edited by Meic Stephens. They were titled, *Cydymaith i Lenyddiaeth Cymru* (Companion to the Literature of Wales). Among those from Liverpool who were invited to contribute were R Merfyn Jones, Patricia Williams and myself. Among the entries I compiled, the one that gave me a great deal of joy was the one on the Liverpool Welsh community, in particular its history and its rich contribution to Welsh literature

■ *John Glyn Davies (1870-1953), poet and scholar who was born in Liverpool and who became , in 1907 a colleague of Dr Kuno Meyer at the University of Liverpool Celtic Department. He became the head of the Department between 1920 and 1936*

and culture. I noted with sadness that the Celtic Department at the University of Liverpool had been closed after all the research and lecturing associated with its directors, such as J Glyn Davies, Idris Foster, Melville Richards and D Simon Evans, each of one whom had enriched Welsh scholarship and letters. During the tenure of D Simon Evans, in the late 1960s and early 1970s, the department had a large number of students and it was a joy to minister to them and to draw them into Welsh activities such as the celebration of the St David's Day Festival on March 1st at Heathfield Road Presbyterian Church of Wales.

NLW

■ *T Gwynn Jones (1871-1949) who was inspired by the Liverpool Welsh historian, Sir JE Lloyd and who himself spent, a period in Liverpool as a journalist*

A founder member of Family Link

Reverend Dafydd Hughes-Parry of Woolton, was a minister, schoolmaster and a leader in the cultural life of the Liverpool Welsh. He was born on 30 September 1930 at Abersoch on the Llŷn peninsula, the son of Elizabeth Jane Parry (from Bont, Llanbrynmair) and Hugh Hughes-Parry, a native of Penrhos, near Pwllheli. He attended Pwllheli Grammar School and the University of Wales, Bangor, where he gained a BA and BD. Ordained a minister of the Presbyterian Church of Wales, he served in that capacity at Maesgeirchen near Bangor. He and his wife Nan (a native of Garndolbenmaen, Caernarfonshire) moved to Liverpool in 1960, and had three daughters, Nia, Mair and Eirian, born in the city.

Dafydd taught at Princes Park School, Highfield and Toxteth and Gateacre Comprehenswive School, and was very active in the social and practical life of the schools. He gave of his best as President of the Welsh Club and arranged for marvellous choirs to the Philharmonic Hall from North and South Wales. Also he was one of the founders of the Family Link (whose offices are now in Anfield) and played an active part in the life of the Welsh Presbyterian Chapels of South Liverpool. His untimely death at Broadgreen Hospital after an operation was a severe loss to the Liverpool

■ *Reverend Dafydd Hughes-Parry*

Welsh community. It took place on 14 May 1987, and the service of thanks-giving was held at Bethel Chapel, Heathfield Raod (where he had been an elder) and the burial at Allerton Cemetery.

Professor of Medicine at King Saud University

Professor David Alan Price Evans, FRCP, has distinguished himself in Saudi Arabia as well as Britain and the USA. Son of Owen and Ellen (née Jones) Evans, he was born in Birkenhead and educated at the University of Liverpool and Johns Hopkins University in the USA. He was given a Personal chair in Medicine at the University of Liverpool in 1968, became Chairman of the Department of Medicine, and from 1965 to 1983 was consultant physician at the Royal Liverpool Hospital and Broadgreen Hospital.

In 1983 he became Director of Medicine at the Riyadh Armed Forces Hospital in Saudi Arabia, and since 1988 he has been an Honorary Professor of Medicine at King Saud University in Riyadh. An international medical academic, he has gained honours and awards at several universities. Since 1972, he has been a life Member of Johns Hopkins Society of Scholars and since 1983 Scientific Editor of the *Saudi Medical Journal*. He enjoys country pursuits, membership of the Welsh Chapel of Bethel, Heathfield Road, and is known in the National Eisteddfod of Wales by his bardic name of Dafydd Paradwys (David of Paradise). Paradwys is the area of Anglesey, near Llangristiolus, where he spends some of his precious holidays.

He was awarded an MSc degree at the University of Liverpool for research on *Experimental Peptic Ulcer* in 1957, and then his MD at the same University in 1959 for research into *Human Isoniazid Metabolism*. In 1965 he was awarded a PH D for research into *Blood Group Substance Metabolism*. DA Price Evans was awarded the Samuel Prize for the PH D Thesis. Earlier at the University of Liverpool he gained a large number of distinctions and prizes. For example he gained the John Hill Abram Prize in Medicine (1951); Sir Robert Kelly Memorial in Surgery (1951); Henry Briggs Memorial Medal in Obstetrics and Gynaecology (1951); Owen T Williams Prize (Highest Aggregate Final MB) (1951); and NE Roberts Prize for the MD Thesis in 1960.

The life and work of Corwena Roberts of Whiston

Corwena Roberts hailed from Llanrwst in the Conwy Valley, where she was born – one of the eight children of Mr and Mrs John Richard Jones of Bod Corwerth. She was educated at the local school and then at the famous Grammar School. After completing her secondary education she went to Bradford to train as a nurse. It was a very interesting period for her, as she became friendly with Menna Jones, from Ysbyty Ifan, who became a missionary nurse in Shillong and later wife of the Reverend T B Phillips of Eglwys Bach. She offered herself as a candidate for the Mission Field in North East India, but she was refused on medical grounds. Deeply disappointed at the decision of the Presbyterian Church of Wales Mission Committee, she returned to Llanrwst with the intention of training as a teacher.

In the meantime she met and married Mostyn Roberts, a ship engineer in Liverpool, and a native of Whiston near Prescot. They lived for a while at Nantlle when Mostyn Roberts had a job as an engineer in one of the valley's quarries. But the attraction of the city and the call of the sea prompted their return to Liverpool, and they made their home in Whiston.

Corwena Roberts involved herself in the life of the area, in particular the Welsh Presbyterian Chapel at Whiston where her father-in-law Moses Roberts had been elected an elder in 1915. She was also elected an elder.

She had an excellent relationship with the thoughtful youngsters of the area and influenced many of them. Mrs Roberts saw the decline in the life of the Welsh chapels of the area, and had to change her spiritual home on three occasions; after the closure of Whiston Chapel she went to Huyton Quarry, and from there to St Helens Junction and finally to Runcorn Welsh Chapel. She extended the hand of friendship to the sick by visiting hundreds of Welsh people in Liverpool hospitals, and in particular the Burns Unit at Whiston Hospital. A daughter, Marian, was born to her. Mrs Roberts suffered for a long time from ill health, but was always full of enthusiasm whenever we visited her at her home. She died on 26 August 1989 and was taken back to the Seion Chapel Cemetery in Llanrwst. The service was conducted by Reverend Dr Goronwy Prys Owen, the minister of the Seion Chapel and by Reverend Arthur Jones, a native of the town and a friend of the family.

Welsh not Scouse

Fritz Spiegl in *Lern Yerself Scouse,* Liverpool, (1990) writes:

> *"It should not be (but is) necessary to say that not all Merseysiders speak Scouse. Some come from places like Llanbrynmair or Llanfaircaereinion or Penrhyndeudraeth and are able to pronounce a mysterious foreign word like ____ ."*

I will not reprint the word used by Spiegl. But he has a very valid point. Welsh is heard on the streets of Liverpool, less in 1990 than in 1890 but still heard, and Anne Robinson complained in 2001 of the Welsh pressure in her childhood years in Crosby and Liverpool (around 1950?) Classes are held in the language though Liverpool has never had a

■ *Robin Huw Bowen with his triple harp*

■ *Robin with his parents Mona and Evan Bowen (West Derby)*

Welsh language school. Some of us tried to establish one in the early 1970s but we were unsuccessful. Still, some of our young people have become very fluent on radio and television, such as Gwenan Ellis Roberts, Sian

■ *The centenery of the famous University of Oxford Welsh Society, Cymdeithas Dafydd ap Gwilym, and in this remarkable photograph, there are three Liverpool welshmen, Reverend Aled Davies, Iolo Llywelyn (Llanrug) and Dafydd Ll. Rees.*

Pari Huws, Dafydd Llywelyn Rees, Owain Ellis Roberts as presenters and producers, Robin Huw Bowen, Peryn Clement-Evans and Huw Clement-Evans as entertainers, and Gareth Thomas as a Westminster politician. It is a credit to their homes and their chapel communities.

■ *Young people of the Welsh community in Otterspool in the early 1980s*

Dr John G Williams

■ *Children and young people of Bethel Chapel near Penny Lane*

A Welsh Childhood: Alice Thomas Ellis

In 1990 Anna Haycroft, who also calls herself Alice Thomas Ellis, published in London her autobiography *A Welsh Childhood*. She was born in Liverpool and is highly critical of contemporary Liverpool:

> *"Liverpool 8, where my family lived, was a truly neighbourly district where everyone knew everyone else. It is now known as Toxteth and the atmosphere is entirely changed."*

"Brookside" the television soap opera which began in 1982, irritates her:

> *"...watching "Brookside" I feel rather as a Sioux warrior might feel if he had survived long enough to watch, say "L A Law" – baffled, resentful and wild with regret for the Good Old Days."*

"Brookside" does not give Liverpool a very good image, for those who live on the Close are at each other's throats from one session to the next. The accent is artificial, not the authentic one which, as Anna Haycroft points out, is derived in equal parts from Welsh, Irish, English and catarrh. Alice Thomas Ellis left Liverpool, but she identifies herself very much with the city in the days when the Celtic influence was so obvious. She writes:

> *"People now think of it mainly as the home of the Beatles, God Help Us. I prefer to remember it as the home of people like my Uncle Percy, who played second violin in the Philharmonic all his life and hated music."*

■ *Welsh Children from Waterloo Chapel*

A tribute to John Henry Roberts *(Monallt)*

A fine strict metre poet who practised his art in the Liverpool of the interwar years, John Henry Roberts was born in Llanberis, Caernarfonshire in 1900 and spent his early days at Bodedern, Anglesey. After the death of his father in 1913, he came to Liverpool, and finally found work in a cotton warehouse. He became part of the Liverpool Welsh Bardic Circle, attending Edge Lane Calvinistic Methodist Chapel, where he came across poets like William Morgan (Collwyn) and R Lloyd Jones. He also became friends with William Edwards (Gwilym Deudraeth) and Robert Parry (Madryn). In the company of these gifted men he mastered the poetic metres. His son Emrys was born just after the National Eisteddfod of Wales in Liverpool in 1929, and was given his name in tribute to the winning poet for the, Awdl (Ode) Dewi Emrys. He returned to Wales at the beginning of the Second World War, conscious of the risk to life of staying in the city and made his home with his wife and family at Penrhyndeudraeth, Merionethshire. There he earned his living as a roadman working for the County Council, and befriended some local characters including the bibliophile Bob Owen (Croesor) (1885-1962) whom he captures in an *"englyn"* of distinction. Monallt, as he was known in Eisteddfodic circles, died in 1991.

■ *Robert Parry (Madryn) on St David's Day, 1933*

The minister's son: H Justin Evans

Howell Justin Evans overcame numerous difficulties and in his lifetime became a great ambassador of

■ *The children of Garston Welsh Chapel*

youth and sport. Born to a Welsh Presbyterian manse in Garston, Liverpool, he never forgot the efforts and sacrifices of his parents on behalf of himself and his brothers. His father, Reverend J D Evans, ministered at the chapel in Chapel Road, for forty-two years and Justin Evans was born there in 1903. He was educated at a private Methodist school in Garston and at Liverpool Institute High School from 1913-1922, but during that period he was out of education for over two years because of ill health.

He left the Institute for a job in a shipping office. But his great ambition was to enter Oxford and, through the generous financial support of the Unitarian ship-owner Sir Sidney Jones, he was able to achieve that ambition. He studied Greats at University College Oxford, which his sons, Hugh and Gareth also later attended. Gareth became a Fellow of University College and his premature death in 1980 was a devastating blow to his parents and an irreplaceable loss to the world of philosophy.

After graduating at Oxford in 1930 Justin Evans returned to his native city. His first post there was as Assistant Warden at the Liverpool University settlement in Nile Street and Warden of York House Boys' Club. Over the years I have met many of those who attended that club and they all have tremendous regard for his initiative, eadership and dynamism. In 1936 he vas appointed Secretary for Training of he National Association of Boys' Clubs. His work made him a well-known figure throughout Britain and was recognized in 1942 by the award of the MBE for his services to youth. In that year he married Gwladus Tudor Davies of Llangollen. They were to have two sons and two daughters.

In May 1944 Justin Evans was appointed Deputy Secretary of the Central Council for Physical Recreation (CCPR) and for the next twenty-four years he gave distinguished service to the movement. He also became the historian of the movement and his book, a biographical tribute to Phyllis Colson, who inspired the formation of CCPR, was published in 1974 under the title, *Service to Sport: The Story of CCPR 1935-1972*. It tells the fascinating story of the CCPR from its formation until its staff and assets were transferred to the Sports Council and later the Sports Councils of Wales and Northern Ireland on their establishment as statutory bodies. Justin Evans had a great deal of interest and influence in the institution of National Recreation Centres and as the leading figure in the setting up of the

E. Emrys Jones

■ *Garston Chapel in Chapel Road*

well-known mountaineering centre of Plas-y-Brenin (King's House) at Capel Curig in Snowdonia. It was characteristic of him that, years later in 1954, he arranged a meeting of mountain centre wardens and

◀ *Another site of a Welsh Presbyterian Chapel in Garston. This Chapel had all its services in English while all the services of the Chapel Road Sanctuary were in the Welsh language.*

other administrators and from this initiative developed the Mountain Leadership Board.

■ *Garston Chapel through the lens of E Emrys Jones*

Justin Evans's name will also be associated with the Wolfenden Report, *Sport and the Community.* He was Secretary of the Wolfenden Committee on Sport (1957-1960), whose recommendations led to the establishment of the first national Sports Council in 1965 and persuaded the Harold Wilson's Labour Government to appoint a Minister for Sport.

In February 1965, Justin Evans was appointed Acting General Secretary of CCPR, a position he held until his retirement in 1968. He proved himself in that period, as he had done throughout his life's work, a man of courage with a fine, precise, logical mind and a most capable colleague. He was awarded the OBE for his services to physical recreation in his retirement year.

He and his supportive wife, Gwladus decided to move back to a delightful spot, Church Stretton, on the England-Wales border and for the next twenty-two years he enjoyed his home, his friends and writing, often on matters concerned with youth and Welsh affairs, to the letter columns of the Liverpool *Daily Post* and *The Times.* Fond of music (in his early years he was a very able organist), he busied himself with local matters, the Civic Society and conservation work. A staunch Liberal (a member of the National Liberal Club), he was well-known in youth and sports circles, and his first book *First Steps in Club Leadership,* published in 1938, is still a useful guide and has now reached its tenth edition. He was editor of *Physical Recreation* from 1949 to 1958. He died on 12 February 1992 in Shrewsbury.

A tribute to Laura Myfanwy Jones

Laura Myfanwy Jones was a headmistress and Education Adviser to the City of Liverpool. She was born at Tiber Street, Toxteth on 20 October 1890, to William and Laura Jones (née Roberts), who had six children in all. Her father was from the Pentir/Rhiwlas area and her mother from Bryncir, a village on the main road between Caernarfon and Porthmadog. Her mother died at the age of ninety-five in 1956. It was a close-knit family. Richard, the eldest child died in 1958, Nell died in 1953, Margaret died on December 21st just before Christmas 1973 and Winifred Ann Jones died on Good Friday 1989. Elizabeth Ann died at eleven months in 1889.

Laura M Jones was educated at Liverpool and also at St Mary's College, Bangor. In 1913, the year of their father's death, she and her brother shouldered responsibility for the family. Webster Road Welsh Presbyterian Chapel where her father was a precentor, was the spiritual home of the family. She received support from Reverend William Owen, who ministered there from 1896 until 1915 and allowed her to borrow books from his own personal library. In her childhood she spend several weeks of her holidays at Bryncir. She took after her grandmother, who lived to the age of ninety-nine.

Laura Jones spent her whole career in the service of the Education Authority of Liverpool as a teacher, deputy headmistress, and headmistress. When a new school was opened in Finch Lane in 1933 she was given the responsibility of making a success of it as headmistress. It was no wonder that she was appointed Adviser to the Liverpool Schools and an agent for attracting many Welsh men and women as teachers from Bangor Normal College and St Mary's College Bangor to the schools of the authority.

She was an exceptional individual. Along with a clear mind, she possessed an enduring personality. She was fortunate that after losing her sister in 1989, she was able to stay at her home through the care given to her by so many of her friends. Miss Laura M Jones was a wonderful member of the Presbyterian Church of Wales, Heathfield Road, an influence on generation after generation of children. She died on Wednesday morning, 18 August 1993 at Broadgreen Hospital after a short illness. A service of thanksgiving was held on Monday morning August 23rd at Bethel Chapel, Heathfield Road, Liverpool and then at Springwood Crematorium, and her casket was placed in the family grave at Smithdown Cemetery, Toxteth.

The portrait of a surgeon: Wil Lloyd Jones

■ *Wil Lloyd Jones*

One of the most popular surgeons of the post-war period in Liverpool is Wil Lloyd Jones whose expertise has assisted thousands at Broadgreen and Lourdes Hospitals in particular. A native of Parc in the heart of Anglesey, Wil Lloyd Jones is in the great tradition of the Liverpool Welsh surgeons. I was privileged to christen his two daughters, Angharad and Tristan, and to be his minister for the last thirty-two years.

He is steeped in the history of his country and has a delightful command of the Welsh language and its literature.

A Vice-President of the Liverpool Welsh Choral Union, Wil Lloyd Jones enjoys their concerts at the Philharmonic Hall. He has his offices at Rodney Street and at Lourdes Hospital, resides in Liverpool but loves to travel, to lecture and to visit other health centres in Europe and the USA. Highly regarded in his profession this unassuming surgeon is worthy of praise for his dedication and commitment to medicine.

Roy Watterson of Liverpool and Australia

At the National Eisteddfod of Wales in Abergele in 1995 the Welsh in exile were led to the Annual Ceremony by a Liverpudlian, Roy Watterson of Balmain East, New South Wales, Australia. He was born on 24 February 1935 at 20 Bloom Street, one of ten children. His parents spoke English, though his mother's family had their roots in Caernarfonshire. Roy was only six when he moved with other members of the family as evacuees to Llansannan near Hiraethog mountain. He refused to return to Liverpool with his brothers Fred and Alf and sisters Pauline and Josei at the end of the war. To him, Marged Evans of Chwibren Isaf in Llansannan was a devoted mother and he remained with her. He was

■ *Hiraethog Mountain known as the Denbigh Moors*

being enriched in the local chapel, called after the 19th Century Liverpool Welsh preacher, Henry Rees. The minister, Reverend Robert Owen, a socialist and hymn-writer, immersed him in Welsh culture. When he did finally return to Liverpool he joined Bill West's Harmony Boys, and then in 1952 emigrated to Australia. Since 1986 he has been arranging for Welsh Male Voice Choirs to visit 'down under', and getting packed venues for such outstanding choirs as the Llanelli Male Voice Choir.

■ *Hiraethog Mountain which gave the Liverpool Welsh polymath William Rees (1802-1883) his bardic name od Gwilym Hiraethog*

A biography of Dr R Arthur Hughes

Dr Robert Arthur Hughes, the medical missionary in Shillong, India from 1939-1969, was born on 3 December 1910 in Oswestry, Shropshire, a market town on the borders of Wales and England. His father, Reverend Howel Harris Hughes, came from a Liverpool Welsh family and Oswestry (Oswald Road Chapel) was his second pastorate. The mother, Annie Myfanwy (née Davies) hailed from Garth near Acrefair and had been a headmistress in Rhosllanerchreugog. They moved as a family from the borderlands to Bangor and he received most of his elementary education at Garth School. From Tabernacle Welsh Calvinistic Methodist Chapel his father moved to the Welsh Chapel in Waterloo, north Liverpool and he and his twin brother received their education at Christchurch and the Grammar School of Waterloo near Seaforth (1921-1925) before they moved to Llandudno, where he received schooling in the famous John Bright School.

Dr Hughes had a notable career in the Faculty of Medicine of the University of Liverpool, which he entered in 1928. Awarded a Gold Medal in Surgery, he qualified in 1933. Then he was appointed as house surgeon to the Liverpool Welsh Presbyterian elder Mr (later Professor) O Herbert Williams, and house physician to Dr (later Professor) Norman Capon at the Royal Southern Hospital, Liverpool. Later he was appointed John Rankin Fellow in Human Anatomy at the university before spending two years at the David Lewis Northern Hospital as surgical tutor, pathologist and registrar. After being accepted with great joy by the Executive Committee of the Welsh Mission he gained an added qualification in Tropical Medicine at the University of London as well as having further training at the Radium Institute and Mount Vernon Hospital.

At the David Lewis Northern Hospital he met a young nursing sister, Nancy (Ann Beatrice) Wright from Heswall in the Wirral. They were married on 7 January 1939 and set sail from Birkenhead on 28 January 1939. Dr Hughes's arrival in Shillong (symbolically he commenced his duties on March 1st, St David's Day) meant everything to the Reverend Dr Hugh Gordon Roberts, the founder of the hospital, who had been a missionary with his beloved wife Katie since 1913. The Shillong Hospital had established an enviable reputation since its opening in 1922. Dr Hughes built on this foundation, even improving it through his dedication and skill. He took charge of all the general wards whilst Reverend Dr Roberts continued with the administration, and on the Reverend's retirement in 1942, he became the Senior Medical Officer, Administrator and Finance Officer.

As if that was not enough he was seconded for service as a liaison officer between the Indian Army, the Assam Government, Civil Health Authorities, British Army Forces and the Tea Industries Medical Services dealing with the recruited labour forces working on the widening of the road from Kohima to Dimapur – the famous Burma Road – during the evacuation of civilian refugees when the Japanese bombed Imphal. Dr Hughes was involved in treating the wounded at the Dimapur Refugee Camp before being posted back to Shillong to serve as the surgeon to the Military Hospital, the British Military Hospital and the Welsh Mission Hospital a total of fifteen hundred beds. This continued from 1942 to 1945, by which time 2,851 officers and soldiers from all

over the world, many from his own denomination and fellow Welshmen, were treated by him, over and above the usual case load.

The Welsh Mission Hospital under Dr R Arthur Hughes and his staff became one of India's greatest hospitals, comparable to St Luke's Hospital in Hiranpur, Bihar, drawing patients from all parts of India.

Above all, Dr Arthur Hughes will be remembered as the medical pioneer. His achievements were extraordinary. He was the first surgeon to introduce 'laser segment caesarean section' before the days of antibiotics. When his assistant Dr Drinsing, whom he instructed in the technique before putting him in charge of the maternity ward, wrote an article for the *Christian Medical Journal* on their experiences in Shillong, it emerged that this was a first not only in Assam but in the whole of the Indian subcontinent. Dr Hughes was the first to introduce vagus nerve resection in the treatment of duodenal ulcer in Assam; he introduced the Oxford Ether Vaporiser into general anaesthesia in North East India and recognized rickets in the infant population as well as the protein calorie deficiency called kwashiorkor, developing the same principles for its treatment.

With the hospital as his base, the next step for Dr Hughes was to determine as factually as possible the medical needs in the countryside, and to this end he organized a number of scientific enquiries and sociological surveys. One such tour of about ninety miles on foot, was made into the villages of the Bhoi in 1947, and he followed a previously-devised plan to collect information in each village by examining each child and questioning each mother. This knowledge was then presented by Dr Hughes and his helpers to the villagers in a village *"durbar"* on the evening following the end of each tour, for he believed that statistics of this kind were of greatest significance to the villagers themselves. The figures were appalling. Infantile mortality rates of about three hundred per thousand were the least bad they found, and in some villages the rate reached five hundred by the age of ten or twelve. Every child over the age of six months had an enlarged spleen, for the area was one of hyperendemic

malaria. Dr Hughes realized that if malaria and dysentery could be controlled then infant and child mortality would be drastically reduced. In addition gross evidence of malnutrition, marasmus, rickets, kwashiorkor, anaemia and goitre abounded, and it seemed that vitamin A deficiency was possibly the commonest cause of blindness among the young.

Dr Hughes and his supportive wife Nancy left Shillong and retired from India on 16 May 1969. Two days earlier the citizens of Shillong met in a farewell party with the hillsmen of Khasia present in their hundreds. He had become a living legend. They came to pay their homage to a missionary who had brought them the blessing of medicine and the Gospel, for he had been elected an elder in 1944 and played his full part in the life of the Presbyterian Church at Mawkhar. When the doctor rose to reply he had to halt frequently for he did not want to leave Shillong and in the subsequent twenty-seven years he spent in Liverpool he was daily in communication by letter, 'phone conversations, references in his sermons, comments and prayers in the monthly Monday missionary prayer meetings as well as welcoming Khasi men and women to his home to stay and re-live the years of service.

After arriving back in Liverpool, he was appointed Sub-Dean in the Faculty of Medicine. His colleague, Professor T Cecil Gray said of him in an obituary:

> " He was a pioneering Sub-Dean in that he strongly encouraged in situ training in general practice years before this became generally accepted."

In 1984 Dr Hughes was asked to go back to Shillong Hospital to help in a difficult situation, and in 1991 he and Nancy, with others from the mother church, visited the celebrations for the one hundred and fiftieth anniversary of the coming of the Gospel to the Khasi Hills with the arrival of Thomas Jones. It gave him great joy to open a new building in the Ri Lyngngan and to take part in the open air service at the golf course on Sunday afternoon before a congregation estimated at a quarter of a million.

He was honoured in his own Welsh Presbyterian Church at Liverpool,

elected an elder at Heathfield Road Chapel in 1971, and later the church Secretary, elected Moderator of the Liverpool Presbytery and finally invited to be the Moderator of the Presbyterian Church of Wales. His twin brother, Reverend John Harries Hughes was elected Moderator at the General Assembly held in Liverpool in 1975, whilst his other brother Dr Arthur Hughes was nominated as Moderator-elect at another Liverpool-based General Assembly in 1991.

Despite coronary problems he survived until 1 June 1996. He died at the Cardiothoracic Centre in Broadgreen Hospital, Liverpool, a city with which he had strong connections from his father and grandparents.

His lasting memorials as a surgeon are the hospital at Shillong and an excellent Souvenir Volume published in Shillong in 1997, and it was most fitting that Dr Pherlock Lamare, who occupies his post today, should travel all the way to his funeral at Bethel Heathfield Road Presbyterian Church of Wales, Liverpool, on Monday 10 June 1996.

The life and work of the Reverend John Meirion Lloyd

Missionary and Principal of the Theological School in Aijawl, John Meirion Lloyd was born in the slate-quarrying town of Corris, Merionethshire on 4 May 1913 to a family involved in that industry and a brother of his Dr R Glynne Lloyd, became a minister of the Presbyterian Church in Ferndale, Heathfield Road, Liverpool and in Utica, USA.

J M Lloyd was naturally gifted academically and gained BA and BD degrees at the University of Wales and a Diploma in Education at the University of Birmingham. Accepted to the Welsh Mission field of North East India, on 17 September 1940, and ordained in Swansea on 5 November 1941, he was unable to reach his destination for some years because the ships sailing there were full of soldiers. He spent most of the war years in the service of the Student Christian Movement in South Wales and as minister of the Presbyterian Chapel at Catharine Street, Liverpool, which later moved to St Columba's, Smithdown Road. It was in this period that he met Joan and they were married in Liverpool.

After his long wait, he was given five days to prepare for sailing on the ship called *"Stirling Castle"*. There were hundreds of missionaries from every part of Britain on that ship and mostly from the Protestant denominations. He himself declared in his *book "Y Bannau Pell: Cenhadaeth Mizoram (The Far Peaks:* the Mission) published by the Presbyterian Church of Wales, Caernarfon, 1989:

"It is possible that no boat ever sailed to India with more missionaries on it."

J M Lloyd with another missionary, a native of Criccieth, Gwen Rees Roberts, sailed to India and he was appointed Headmaster of Aijawl High School for Boys. It only had sixty-six pupils in 1945, but many of the young people of Lushai had been awaiting patiently for this golden opportunity. Most of the children came to school barefoot and had a great thirst for knowledge. By 1947 the buildings were quite inadequate but, with help from MacDonald, President of Mizoram (which is situated in North East India) a new school was ready by 1949. This was the year Meirion Lloyd and his family could have a furlough and a new native headmaster was appointed as his successor.

When Lloyd returned to Lushai he was appointed Principal of the Theological School of Mizoram. It was a small school then but under his guidance it grew year after year with never a break. They followed the syllabus of the Serampore Theological College. Though the school was not fully accredited, it was there that a number of very talented men who were to become church leaders began their studies. The synod were keen that the ministerial students should have every opportunity and a large number received further tuition at Cherra, Serampore, and even as far afield as Bangalore. The Scottish theologian and commentator William Barclay arranged that his valuable New Testament commentaries could be purchased by the students at a reasonable rate.

J M Lloyd did a great deal for education in Mizoram. He also belonged to the panel of scholars who translated the Old Testament into the Mizo language and ensured a complete Bible for the inhabitants of Mizoram. The translation was completed on 26 August 1955 and meetings of celebration were held at Serkawn, Lwnglei and Aizawl, but the people had to wait another four years before receiving the first edition because of the inability of the Bible

Society's Office at Chowringhee, Calcutta to cope with the demand.

Meirion Lloyd took an abiding interest in the early history of the Welsh Mission, and wrote *Ar Bob Bryn Uchel* an account of the pioneers (published in 1952), with an English Edition, *On Every High Hill* following in 1956. Then he wrote on the missionary D E Jones, *Arloesydd Lushai - Hanes D E Jones* (London 1958).

In his retirement he was very active writing a detailed account of the mission work, *Y Bannau Pell: Cenhadaeth Mizoram* (see above) and editing a useful paperback volume, *Nine Missionary Pioneers: the story of nine pioneering missionaries* (Caernarfon, 1989).

He returned to Liverpool in 1964, served the Bible Society as an area representative for ten years and became a member of the Welsh Presbyterian Chapel of Heathfield Road near Penny Lane. He was a great asset to the Welsh and English chapels. Then he undertook the pastorate of a United Reformed Church in Rhyl (1977-1978) before retiring in 1978 and moving with his wife to Prestatyn. J M Lloyd died in 1997.

A welcome to Llanelli Male Voice Choir

In the first few months of 1998 the executive committee of the Welsh language community newspaper *Yr Angor (The Anchor),* under the chairmanship of E Goronwy Owen with the wholehearted support of the conscientious secretary Ken Williams (Gateacre), the treasurer Ron Gilford (Cheadle), myself as editor and all the members (Marian Prys Davies (Childwall), Mair Jones (Childwall), Anne Jones (Bebington), Lois Murphy (Manchester), Arthur Edwards (Aigburth), Hywel Jones (Barnston), H Wyn Jones (Allerton), Walter Rees Jones (Birkenhead), Alan Morris (Runcorn) and William Evans (Anfield) - and since 2000 Reverend W R Williams and Mrs Menna Williams (Manchester)- decided to arrange a concert featuring the Llanelli Male Voice Choir.

The day of the concert arrived, with three coaches coming from Llanelli, and on Saturday 4 July 1998 the large auditorium of Heathfield Road (seating seven hundred and twenty) was packed. It was a huge success. The choir was at its best under the baton of Eifion Thomas and the organist Gethin Hughes. The President of the evening, Professor Huw Rees, and I as compere, expressed our sympathies for the family of his Honour John Edward Jones whose funeral had been held the previous day. I was much surprised when the President of the choir Mr D Hughes Davies of Llanddarog (late of Southport), came on before the end of the concert to invite me to be a Vice-President of the choir. It was a great honour.

■ *Members of the Angor committee in the 1990's*

1998

A biography of Dr E Wyn Jones

kind-hearted, pacifist, remarkable, wise and gifted person, Dr Emyr Wyn Jones gave a lifetime of service to Wales and humanity. The son of Presbyterian Minister, Reverend James Jones, and his wife Ellen Jones, he was born in the Snowdonian village of Waenfawr on 23 May 1907 and educated locally and at Caernarfon County School. From there he proceeded to the University of Liverpool and graduated MB ChB in June 1928 with First Class Honours and Distinctions in medicine and surgery. He was one of the brightest students of his generation according to Sir Robert Kelly, won scholarships and prizes, and produced an important thesis on *"Radiographic Study of the Coronary Arteries"*. In 1938 he joined the staff of the Royal Liverpool Infirmary, where he became Senior Physician and was in charge of the Cardiac Department for over twenty-five years. In addition, he became physician-in-charge of the Liverpool Regional Cardiac Studies Unit at the University. A founder member of the British Cardiac Society in 1937, he was its Chairman in 1968, and served on the Welsh Hospital Board from 1952

until its dissolution in 1974. For twenty years he was consulting physician to the main North Wales Hospitals as well as having a consulting practice to the main North Wales hospitals at Bangor, Rhyl and Wrexham and one in Rodney Street.

■ *Dr Emyr Wyn Jones never missed the Liverpool Welsh Choral Union concerts at the Philharmonic Hall.*

The non-medical aspects of his life made him an extremely busy person in his retirement. He was High Sheriff of the County of Caernarfon in 1974. In the organization of the Royal National Eisteddfod of Wales he held office as Chairman of the Council (1973-1976), President of the Court (1983-1886) and from 1967 until 1987 as chief attendant Druid bearing the *nom de plume* Emry Feddyg (Emyr the Physician). In 1987 he was elected

Cymrawd (Fellow), a rare honour, bestowed on at most two or three in a generation.

■ *The surgery of Owen Thomas and Robert Jones at the end of the century.*

Throughout much of his adult life he contributed to the field of cardiology and the history of medicine and in particular literary and historical research. His first two books were written in memory of his first wife, Enid Wyn Jones, who gave him a daughter and a son and who died at his side on 15 September 1967 from a subarachnoid haemorrhage on a return flight from Australia (see entry for 1967 in this volume). I recently re-read *In Memorium – Enid Wyn Jones* Liverpool (1967) *and Cyfaredd Cof (Memory's Magic)* Liverpool (1970) as I had been invited to write a biographical note on Mrs Jones for the

new Dictionary of National Biography. They are superb. His studies on Henry Tudor, the crucial contribution of poets and warriors of medieval Wales and an assessment of the alleged physical deformities of Richard III are dealt with in *A Kinsman King* (1980), *Yr Anterliwt Goll (The Host Interlude)* (1984), *Bosworth Field and its Preliminaries – A Welsh Retrospect,* Liverpool (1984) and *Ymgripys am y Goron ac Ysgrifau Eraill* (The Quest for a Crown and Other Essays) Bala (1991).

His study of Sir Henry M Stanley in *Sir Henry M Stanley: the Enigma,* Denbigh (1989) and in Welsh, *Henry M Stanley: Pentewyn Tân a'i Gymblethdod Phaetonaidd* (Henry M Stanley: Firebrand and Phaeton) Denbigh (1992) is the most important of his published material, especially for its comments on the explorer's pre-African years, demonstrating conclusively that in his *Autobiography,* Stanley had deliberately distorted the truth, excluded relevant facts and indulged in grotesque inventiveness on

an incredible scale. This research led
to an unravelling for the first time of

E. Emrys Jones

■ *The surgery of Sir Robert Jones in Liverpool, and Dr Emyr Wyn Jones wrote a number of articles on him and on Hugh Owen Thomas.*

Stanley's obscure paternity problem –
hitherto a closely guarded secret for
one hundred and fifty years. In
addition, it became possible to discover
the identify of the pseudonymous
author of Stanley's first biography
(published in 1872) and a revealing
analysis of the explorer's 'porcupine'
personality.

Other studies include books on
medical and literary subjects, *Ar
Ffiniau Meddygaeth (On the
Borderland of Medicine)* 1971,
*Ysgubau'r Meddyg (A physician's
Sheaves)* 1973, *Cyndyn Ddorau ac
Ysgrifau Eraill (Reluctant Doors and
Other Essays)* 1978, his important study
of Dean Shipley and the unearthing of
The Host Interlude of 1784 *in
Diocesan Discord: A Family Affair St*

Asaph 1779-1786, 1988, while his love
for the Lleyn Peninsula can be gleaned
from *Lloffa Yn Llŷn: Trem yn ôl
(Gleanings in Lleyn: A Retrospect)*
1994 and *Y Bysedd Cochion (The
Foxglove)* 1997.

An ardent bibliophile, Dr Jones
acquired many early Welsh printed
books and a useful collection on
Quaker history. Elected a
Presbyterian elder in
Liverpool in 1936, he
subsequently became a
Member of the Society of
Friends, with an abiding
emphasis on pacifism. His
home (from 1942 until
1987) at Llansannan, high
in the hills of Hiraethog,
was a meeting place for
poets, preachers and
musicians. In 1972 he
married Megan, the widow
of Professor T Jones Pierce of
Aberystwyth. In 1987 he removed to a
remote cottage at Rhiw on the tip of
the Lleyn Peninsula, where he enjoyed
himself immensely within sight of the
island and the Sound of Bardsey. He
died in Bangor on 14 January 1999.

E. Emrys Jones

■ *The resting place of the genius of orthoapaedic surgery, Dr Hugh Owen Thomas in Toxteth Cemetary, Smithdown Road.*

A thanksgiving for the life and work of Gwen Vaughan Jones

Dr Henry Cohen (later Lord Cohen of Birkenhead) paid Gwen Tegla Davies (as Gwen Vaughan Jones was known in her nursing days) a rare compliment in a testimonial for her work as a young nurse at the Royal Liverpool Hospital at the beginning of the Second World War:

> *"She proved capable, industrious and knowledgeable, and her attractive and cheerful personality endeared her to the patients under her care. No task was ever too onerous for her."*

Lord Cohen (as the British Medical Association knew well when he was their President) was not a man to waste words and Gwen Tegla Davies lived up to his testimonial for the rest of her life, not least through her complete dedication in the essential role of a volunteer within the National Health Service. She was born in Llanrhaedr-ym-Mochnant, Montgomeryshire on 3 April 1916 and was proud of her middle name, Tegla, for her father, Edward Tegla Davies (1880-1967) was a dissident Welsh Methodist minister of brilliance and his novel, *Gŵr Pen y Bryn (The Man on the Top of the Hill)* published in 1923

is a landmark in Welsh literature. She was the youngest of his three children; her eldest sister married a Labour politician and became Lady Dyddgu Elwyn Jones of Bangor and her late brother Arfon Tegla Davies was the historian of the Friends Ambulance Service which did much sterling service in the World Wars. She embodied so many of the traits, charm, and empathy of Tegla and his wife, Jane Eleanor, who died on 8 May 1948 – the same date as her daughter died in the year 2000. Aldous Huxley would have written a chapter on such a coincidence!

In 1940 she changed her middle name to Vaughan on the occasion of her marriage to Howell Vaughan Jones, the youngest son of the Liverpool builder John William Jones (1865-1945). After the death of his father he became co-director with his four brothers of J W Jones & Sons, a company that built large sections of the huge housing estates of Huyton and Speke. Gwen and Howell (who died in 1979) were a delightful pair – hospitable, gracious, and exceptionally gifted as tennis players. Their annual holidays were spent in towns like Torquay where they could enjoy competitive tennis tournaments. Their involvement in nonconformity and charitable causes endeared them to a large circle of friends. They had one daughter, Nia.

Gwen V Jones became an exceptionally committed hospital visitor and also an outstanding organiser for the League of Friends, in particular at the Women's Hospitals in Catharine Street and later Upper Parliament Street, Liverpool. The rotas for the canteen, shop, trolleys and social events were in her hands, and she was able to persuade numerous women inspired by her charm to work with her. They all admired the long hours of dedicated voluntary service she gave to hospital work. She was honoured in 1999 for her sterling commitment over thirty-five years. In her final decade she suffered from heart disease and osteoporosis and raised large sums for the British Heart Foundation and National Osteoporosis Society.

Her wide experience of dealing with hospital administration, delegating work within the hospital environment and chairing meetings was a bonus. I could add her heart was tender, and her hand generous. She died in Lourdes Hospital, Liverpool on 8 May 2000 and is greatly missed.

◀ *The Women's Hospital in Catherine Street.*

Merseyside Welsh in Photographs

The splendour of Princes Road Presbyterian Church of Wales, Toxteth

E. Emrys Jones

■ *It has been described as the 'most beautiful chapel ever built by the Welsh' (see Y Drysorfa, Volume XL11,437-8)*

■ *A view of the interior of the chapel*

■ *The cost came to £19,633-8-5 in 1865*

■ *The congregation had collected ten thousand pounds by 187*

Another ten Welsh Presbyterian Chapels of Merseyside

■ David Street Welsh Chapel

■ Westminster Road Chapel, Ellesmere Port

■ Webster Road Chapel which was sold in 1925 and became the Cameo Cinema

■ West Kirby Welsh Chapel

■ Fitzclarence Street Welsh Chapel

■ Welsh Chapel, Widnes

Merseyside Welsh in Photographs

■ *Carmel, Bolton Road, Ashton-in-Makerfield*

■ *Belvedere Chapel, Toxteth*

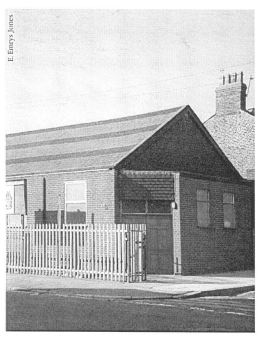

■ *Ramilies Road near Penny Lane*

■ *A sponsored walk by the young people and children on the steps of Bethel Heathfield Road Chapel, Smithdown Place*

A selection of Welsh Chapels which have ceased to be centres for the Welsh settlements.

Welsh Methodist Chapel in Knowsley Road, Bootle

■ *Wavertree Welsh Baptist Chapels*

■ *Spellow Lane Welsh Methodist Chapel*

■ *Tabernacl Welsh Independent Chapel, Belmont Road, Newsham Park*

Woolton Road Independent Chapel (The Welsh congregation moved to the United Reformed Chapel in Lance Lane). It is still known as Tabernacl, Woolton Road, Liverpool

Merseyside Welsh in Photographs

Another female author that remembers her Welsh childhood in Liverpool is Dr Eirwen Meiriona Gwynn (1916-) Her home was in Sheil Road

■ *Eirwen Gwynn's home in Sheil Road, Liverpool in the early 20's*

■ *Eirwen's father, William ST John Williams was a dentist in Sheil Road*

■ *Eirwen Gwynn as a young scientist. She married in 1942 with the Welsh poet, Harri Gwynn (1913-85)*

■ *Another portrait of the prolific writer*

The John Mills family have followed in the footsteps of John Thomas, Cambrian Gallery, the pioneer Liverpool Welsh photographer.

Their present offices in Hope Street

■ *Thomas Mills*

■ *Gwilym Mills*

■ *John C Mills*

■ *Andrew Mills*

Birkenhead Welsh Cultural Activities

■ *Members of the Birkenhead Drama Company*

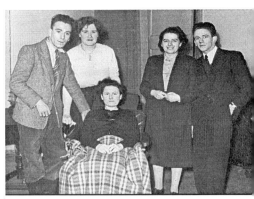

■ *Members of the Birkenhead Drama Company*

■ *Members of the Birkenhead Drama Company*

■ *Members of the Birkenhead Drama Company*

■ *Members of the Birkenhead Drama Company*

■ *Members of the Birkenhead Drama Company*

■ *Members of the Birkenhead Drama Company*

■ *Birkenhead ladies at the Eisteddfod*

■ *Members of the Birkenhead Drama Company*

■ *Members of the Birkenhead Drama Company*

Merseyside Welsh in Photographs

■ *Glenys a Gwynfryn Jones of Anfield*

■ *Mrs Meinwen Rees being presented to Queen Elisabeth II*

■ *Robin Huw Bowen, the Liverpool born Welsh harpist*

■ *Rev David Emrys James 'Dewi Emrys' who won the Chair at the National Eisteddfod of Wales in Liverpool (1929)*

■ *Rev JT Oldfield Davies*

■ *Mrs E J Evans, the wife of the Minister of Walton Park Welsh Chapel*

This book has been well served by:

■ *E Emrys Jones*

■ *John G Williams*

Donations

The following have kindly given a donation towards this volume:

APPENDIX B

A   CHURCHES:

i)   Bethel Heathfield Road Presbyterian Church of Wales, Liverpool 15, as well as the Literary Society of the chapel, the Eisteddfod Choir, the Sunday School and Cylch y Merched.

ii)   Bethania Presbyterian Church of Wales, Crosby Road South, Waterloo.

iii)   Peniel Presbyterian Church of Wales, Portland Street, Southport.

iv)   Liverpool Presbytery of the Presbyterian Church of Wales.

v)   Liverpool and District Welsh Chapels (CECLAC).

B   COMPANIES:

i)   Pearson Collinson Funeral Services Ltd, 87-91 Allerton Road, Liverpool 18.

ii)   Modern Welsh Publications Ltd, Allerton, Liverpool 18.

C   WELSH ORGANISATIONS IN LIVERPOOL

i)   Liverpool Welsh Society (Cymdeithas Cymry Liverpool).

ii)   Cylch Pump ar Hugain.

iii)   Llesau Maesgrug, Liverpool.

iv)   Merseyside Welsh Eisteddfod (Eisteddfod Gadeiriol Glannau Mersi).

D   INDIVIDUALS:

i)   Mr John Derbyshire, Mossley Hall, Liverpool

ii)   Mr Ted Clement-Evans, Woolton, Liverpool

iii)   Mr A T George, London (late of Bootle)

iv)   Mr R Ifor Griffiths, Liverpool

v)   Miss Lilian Hughes, Llanfairfechan, Conwy

vi)   Mr and Mrs R E Jones, Tŷ Croes, Anglesey (Late of Liverpool)

vii)   Dr Gweneth Lilly, Llanfairfechan (late of Liverpool)

viii)   Miss Mair Powell, West Derby, Liverpool

ix)   Reverend Dr D Ben Rees and Mrs Meinwen Rees, Liverpool

x)   Mr Gwilym Roberts, Sussex (late of Waterloo)

xi)   Mr Hywel Heulyn Roberts, Synod, near Llandysul, Ceredigion (late of Liverpool)

xii)   Mr and Mrs Iolo Francis Roberts, Newcastle-under-Lyme, Staffordshire

xiii)   Mr R Alun Roberts and Mrs Gwyneth Roberts, Waterloo, Liverpool

xiv)   Mr Emrys Williams, Ellesmere Port

List of Subscribers

The following have kindly associated themselves with publication of this volume by subscription:

Reverend Kathie Bennett, Knotty Ash, Liverpool
Bethania, Presbyterian Church of Wales, Waterloo, Crosby
Mrs Mona Bowen, West Derby, Liverpool
Mrs Margaret Bradley, Wallasey
Mr Adrian Cohen (Actionstride Ltd)
Mrs Undeg Cole, Swansea
Pearson Collinson Funeral Services Ltd, Allerton, Liverpool
Mr Geoffrey F Crump, Portishead, Bristol
Mr Hywel Rhys Davies, Vancouver, Canada
Mr and Mrs John Davies, Rhuthun, Clwyd
Mr W Hywel Davies, Allerton, Liverpool
Mr William Trefor Davies, Devon
Mr John Derbyshire, Mossley Hill, Liverpool
Mrs Catherine Edwards, Allerton, Liverpool
Reverend Eleri Edwards, Allerton, Liverpool
Mrs Lisa Edwards, Garston, Liverpool
Ellesmere Port Presbyterian Church of Wales
Mr Tecwyn Ellis, Mynytho, Pwllheli, Gwynedd
Mr Ted Clement Evans, Woolton, Liverpool
Mr and Mrs W Meirion Evans, Allerton, Liverpool
Miss Hazel A Formby, Tan-y-Llan, Ysgeifiog, Flintshire
Mr A T George, London, NW16
Mrs Dilys R Glover, Mold, Flintshire
Mr Huw Rhys Griffith, Allerton, Liverpool
Mr Owen Griffiths, Llansadwrn, Anglesey
Mr D K Hughes, West Kirby, Wirral
Mrs Lilian Hughes, Llanfairfechan, Conwy
Reverend Jennifer A Hurd, Mold, Clwyd
Mr David R Jones, Wrexham, Clwyd
Mr and Mrs E Emrys Jones, Colwyn Bay
Mr and Mrs Idris Jones, Ashton in Makerfield
Reverend Fr Ieuan Wyn Jones, Cardiff
Mr John Medwyn Jones, Colwyn Bay

List of Subscribers *(continued)*

Mr John Parry Jones, Petersfield

Mrs L H Jones (Dela) Culcheth, Warrington

Mrs Olwen Jones, Allerton, Liverpool

Mr and Mrs R E Jones, Tŷ Croes, Anglesey

Mr O F G Kilgour, Colwyn Bay

Mr A W Lloyd, Rhuthun, Denbighshire

Mr and Mrs John Lyons, Knowsley Village, Knowsley

MANWEB Plc, Liverpool

Merseyguides Association

HSBC Bank Plc, Dale Street Branch, Liverpool

Captain Hugh Morgan, Birkenhead

Reverend John Morris, Llanddaniel, Anglesey

Miss Margaret Morris, Waterloo, Crosby

Dr O R Morris, Llanddaniel, Anglesey

National Library of Wales, Aberystwyth

Mr E Goronwy Owen, Allerton, Liverpool

Mr J Tudor Owen, Birkenhead

Miss Mair Powell, West Derby, Liverpool

Master Tomos Llywelyn Wyn Rees, London

Master Joshua Ceredig Rees, London

Mr Gwilym Roberts, Sussex

Mr and Mrs Idris Roberts, Allerton, Liverpool

Mrs Maureen Roberts, Gwaenysgor (In Memory of Miss Olwen Morris, Stanley Road, Bootle)

Mair and O Trevor Roberts (Llanowain) Rhuthun, Denbighshire

Mr and Mrs R Alun Roberts, Waterloo, Crosby

Mr D H Rogers, Conwy

Mrs Margaret Rogers, Lydiate

Peniel Presbyterian Church of Wales, Portland Street, Southport

Miss Eunice Thomas, Allerton, Liverpool

Mrs Jane Ann Thomas, Berkshire

WEA Liverpool Branch

Mrs Glenys K Williams, Shere, Surrey (Formerly of Waterloo)

Mr and Mrs Idris Williams, Prenton, Birkenhead

Beryl and Dr John G Willliams, Calderstones, Liverpool

Mrs M Williams, Holyhead, Anglesey

feminine wardrobe

21 beautiful skirts, dresses and tops for you to make

Jinko Matsumoto

Laurence King Publishing

As befits the title of this book, I have created twenty-one specifically "feminine" designs with gentle colors, decorative ribbons, flowery prints, lace, and gathers...
You can add as many or as few of these feminine touches as you wish—it's entirely up to you.
This is a wardrobe that lets you switch between town, party, and resort styles with perfect ease.

I've opted for simple lines and silhouettes with the emphasis on ease of sewing, but the patterns also retain their carefully constructed lines for the sophisticated wearer to enjoy.
The superior, even luxurious, fabrics will make your dress designs all the more original.

Jinko Matsumoto

contents

town

peasant blouse

A folklore inspired piece with loose-fitting sleeves,
to wear in a bloused fashion.  page 46

Pair with an apron dress for a relaxed feel.

sleeveless dress
with bow sash

A sleeveless dress with an A-line silhouette
in a modern printed cotton lawn. ⚞ page 36

bow tie shift

Coordinating striped and plain fabrics sit above and below the ribbon bow. ⚘ page 58

shirred bodice tunic

The tunic length makes an ideal partner for pants. Ribbon-tie
shoulder straps make the size adjustable. 🐕 page 71

checked capelet shift

Use a double-faced 2-ply gauze in contrasting large and
small gingham checks for this caped dress. ⋔ page 56

ruffle shoulder dress

A ruffled A-line dress with a spring-like feel.
Different sized dots give a rhythmic quality to
the cut of the fabric. ⋈ page 39

Wear it under a coat with the ruffles just showing.

draped collar dress

A charming dress with a draped collar and shirttail hem. ☛ page 41.

Pair with a loose shirt for an extra cute look.

party

petal sleeve blouse

Classical styling makes for a pretty
silhouette. The overlapping sleeves are
like flower petals. ❧ page 51

tie-front lacy top

The raglan sleeves are made with a
generous amount of delicate fabric.
Indulge yourself with plenty of fine lace
at the neck and cuffs. ❦ page 44

Wear over the bust for a bare-shouldered dress.

convertible sashed skirt/dress

A one-size-fits-all midi-length skirt. Linen embroidered with silver dots. Wear it with a decorative stole for added effect. ❧ page 70

ribbon shoulder shift

Spice up a basic shift with eye-catching ribbon trim. ✀ page 53

ruffle bodice tunic

This design is shaped to fit around the bust and uses a double-sided fabric with dot and stripe variations. ❦ page 67

scalloped hem dress with draped sleeves

Generously tucked dress with eyelet-lace scalloped hem. Pair with a layered stole for a romantic look. ❦ page 48

giant bow-tie tunic

An A-line blouse in silk seersucker. The large bow looks equally stylish on the front or back.

❦ page 36

resort

handkerchief hem sundress

Take a vacation in this graceful moving dress with a drawstring waist. → page 62

sailor collar hem sundress with pockets

The grosgrain ribbon adds an accent to the handkerchief-cut hemline for a marine look. ➔ page 59

convertible knit yoke dress/skirt

A skirt with rib-knit waist, which allows you to vary the length and mood of your outfit. ➦ page 63

Bring the rib-knit bodice up for a bare-shouldered style.
Pair it with a vest (waistcoat) for a chic look.

striped sundress

A dress which uses plenty of soft fabric and makes a feature of the bust line, with elastic in the back to give a good fit. ➜ page 64

ruffle bodice shift

The four-layer ruffle gives an upbeat mood to this summery dress.
Keep your eye on the balance of the ruffles, watching their positioning
and volume. ❧ page 66

bra-top sundress

Use the ribbon through each side of the bra top to adjust the fit. A maxi-length version is also a favorite of mine. ❥ page 68

sweetheart dress with bow bodice

With a bodice like a bow, this dress has a softly pleated body and sleeves. ➽ page 52

How to make the twenty-one designs

Patterns

The full-scale patterns that come with this book feature four sizes, XS, S, M, and L.

To choose your pattern size, refer to the measurements in the size chart below and find the one that matches your bust measurement.

Size chart				Unit: in
	XS	S	M	L
Bust	30¾ (29⅞ to 31½)	32⅝ (31⅞ to 33½)	34⅝ (33⅞ to 35⅜)	36⅝ (35⅞ to 37⅜)
Waist	23¼	25¼	27⅛	29⅛
Hips	33⅞	35⅜	37	38⅝
Height	62¼ to 64⅝			

Size chart				Unit: cm
	XS	S	M	L
Bust	78 (76 to 80)	83 (81 to 85)	88 (86 to 90)	93 (91 to 95)
Waist	59	64	69	74
Hips	86	90	94	98
Height	158 to 164			

The pattern pieces needed for each design are indicated at the start of the instructions. Simply select the pattern pieces you need from the back of the book.

Copy the patterns onto a separate sheet of paper before you use them.

Be careful to ensure that you pick the right size, and remember to copy over any grain lines, ends of openings, stitch ends, markings, and other such details.

The pattern pieces do not contain seam allowances.

Make sure that you add the necessary seam allowance around the edge when you cut the fabric. Refer to the cutting layouts to work out the measurements for your seam allowances.

There are seven basic patterns

The twenty-one designs are grouped under seven patterns, A through G.

pattern A

An A-line with no sleeves or collar.
A1 is a midi-length dress. A2 has a shorter length, and A3 features a ruffle sandwiched from the neckline partway along the front seams.

Full-scale pattern pieces

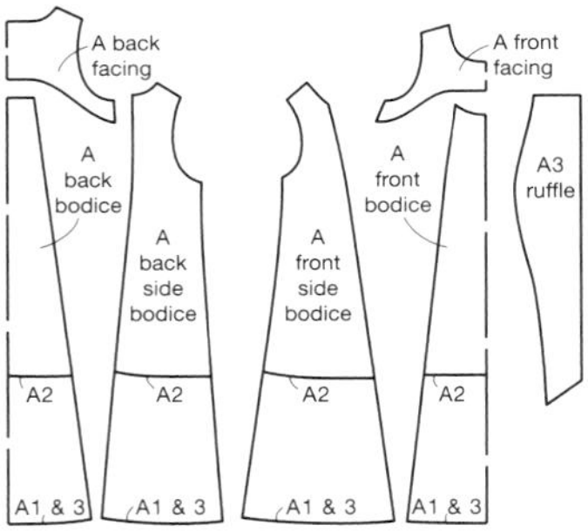

A1
p. 06 dress

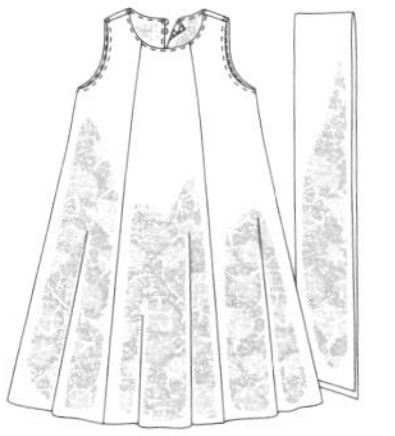

A2
p. 23 tunic

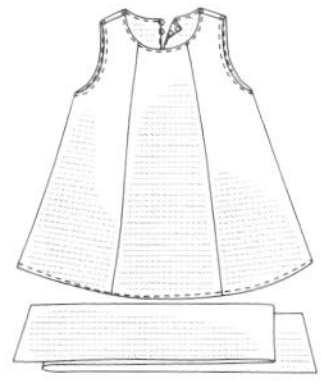

A3
p. 10 dress

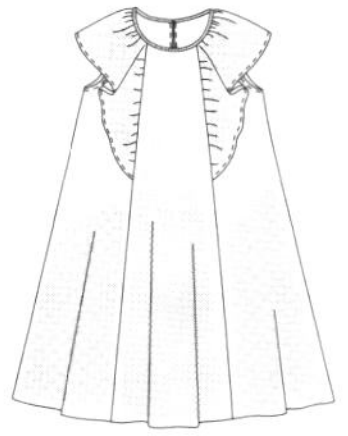

Finished measurements Unit: in

		XS	S	M	L
Bust		35	37	39	41
Length	A1, 3	39 3/8			
	A2	25 5/8			

Finished measurements Unit: cm

		XS	S	M	L
Bust		89	94	99	104
Length	A1, 3	100			
	A2	65			

pattern B

A loose-fitting silhouette with raglan sleeves.
B1 is a loose fitting roll-collar dress. B2 and B3 come in a shorter length, adding a narrow collar band at the neckline. B2 is also decorated with lace, while the waist in B3 is bloused with elastic.

Full-scale pattern pieces

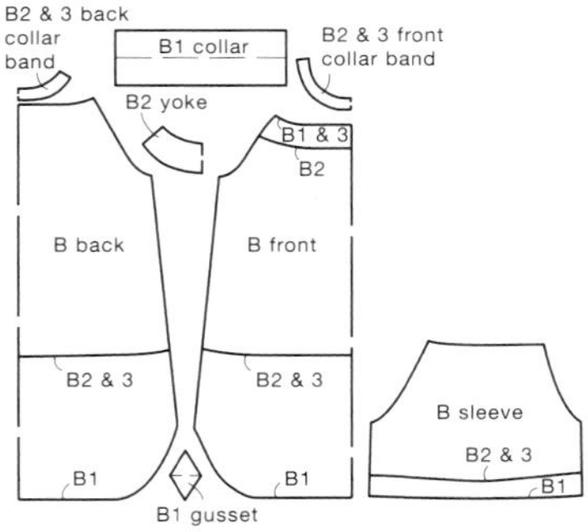

Finished measurements Unit: in

		XS	S	M	L
Bust		49 1/4	51 1/8	53 1/8	55 1/8
Length	B1	39 3/16			
	B2, 3	24 3/8			
Sleeve pattern length	B1	15	15 9/32	15 17/32	15 25/32
	B2, 3	13 3/16	13 15/32	13 23/32	14

Finished measurements Unit: cm

		XS	S	M	L
Bust		125	130	135	140
Length	B1	99.5			
	B2, 3	62			
Sleeve pattern length	B1	38	38.7	39.4	40.1
	B2, 3	33.5	34.2	34.9	35.6

B1
p. 12 dress

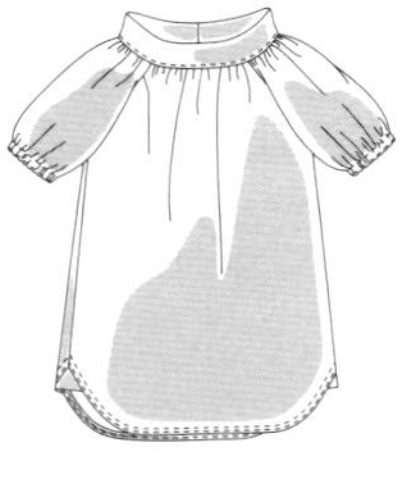

B2
p. 15 lacy top

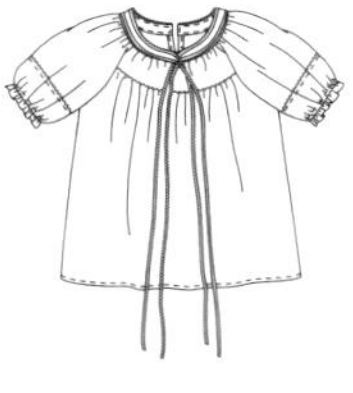

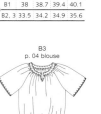

B3
p. 04 blouse

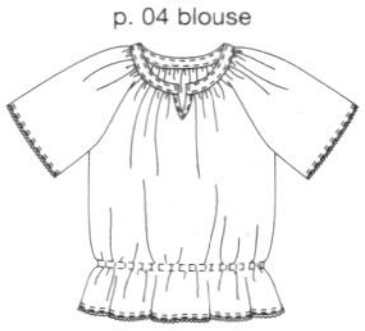

pattern C

Combines a generously tucked bodice with tucked raglan sleeves.
C1 features loose, elbow-length raglan sleeves tied with ribbon through the cuffs. C2 is shorter in length, with small sleeves doubled up for a ruffled effect. C3 adds a bow knot bodice and the sleeves are shorter than C1.

Full-scale pattern pieces

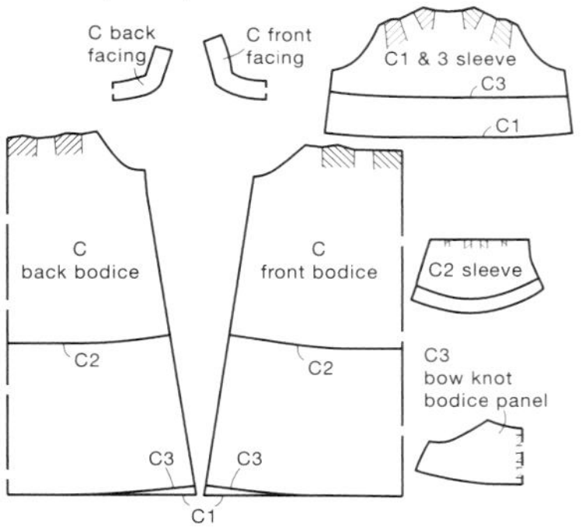

Finished measurements Unit: in

		XS	S	M	L
Bust		33 1/2	35 3/8	37 3/8	39 3/8
Length	C1, 3	37			
	C2	21 7/16			
Sleeve pattern length	C1	13 5/32	13 15/32	13 3/4	14 1/16
	C2	7 1/4	7 1/2	7 25/32	8
	C3	8 17/32	8 13/16	9 1/8	9 17/32

Finished measurements Unit: cm

		XS	S	M	L
Bust		85	90	95	100
Length	C1, 3	94			
	C2	54.5			
Sleeve pattern length	C1	33.4	34.2	35	35.8
	C2	18.3	19	19.7	20.3
	C3	21.7	22.5	23.3	24.1

C1
p. 20 dress

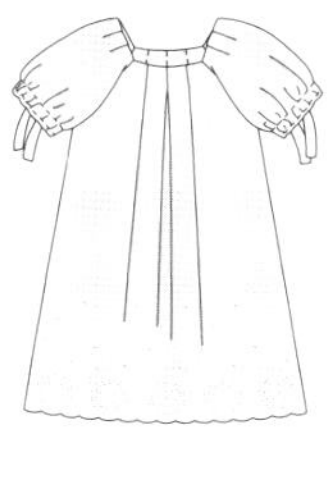

C2
p. 14 blouse

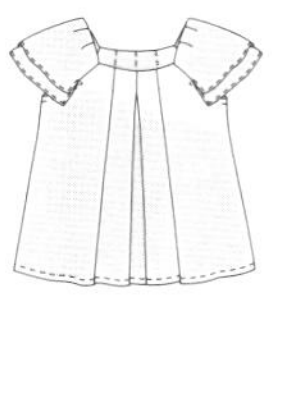

C3
p. 32 dress

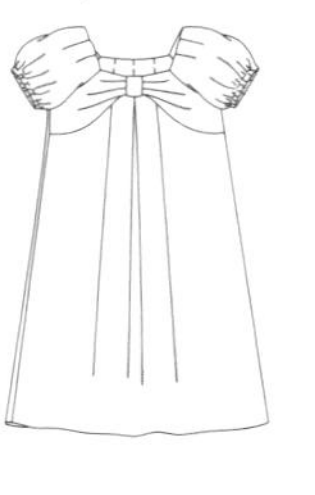

pattern D

A box silhouette dress with ribbon decoration.
D1 has the shoulders tied with ribbons, while D2 features a cape with fine ribbon stitched onto the neckline. In D3 a short, kimono sleeve-style yoke forms a seam at the bust, which is decorated with a bow tie.

Full-scale pattern pieces

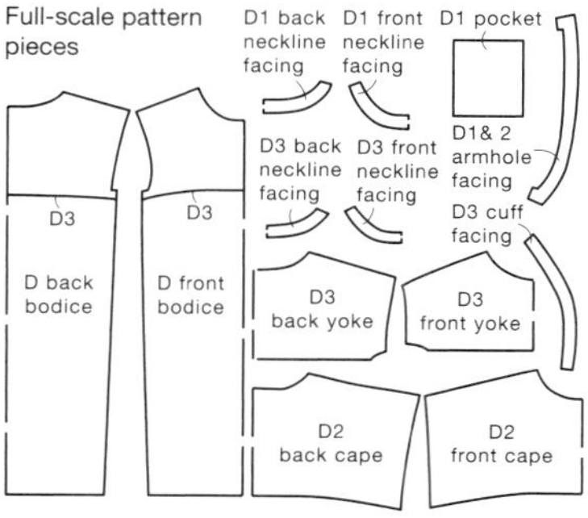

D1 back neckline facing
D1 front neckline facing
D1 pocket
D3 back neckline facing
D3 front neckline facing
D1& 2 armhole facing
D3 cuff facing
D3
D back bodice
D3
D front bodice
D3 back yoke
D3 front yoke
D2 back cape
D2 front cape

Finished measurements — Unit: in

		XS	S	M	L
Bust		39¾	41¾	43¾	45⅝
Length	D1, 2	38 13/16			
	D3				

Finished measurements — Unit: cm

		XS	S	M	L
Bust		101	106	111	116
Length	D1, 2	98.5			
	D3				

D1
p. 18 shift

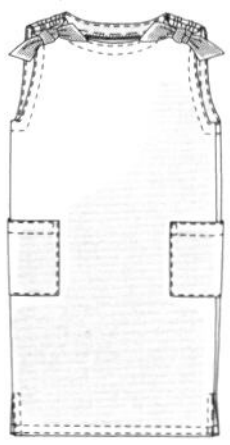

D2
p. 09 shift

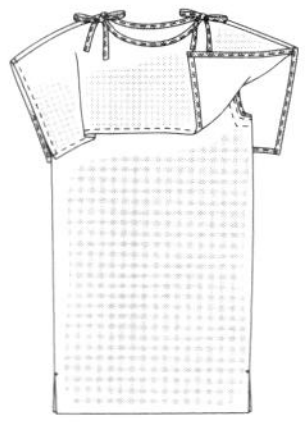

D3
p. 07 shift

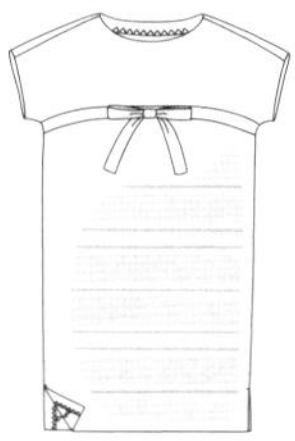

pattern E

These designs have an irregular hemline and use the same pattern piece for the front and back skirts.
E1 and E2 are dresses with a high waist attaching to the bodice. E3 uses a simple tubular rib-knit for the bodice.

Full-scale pattern pieces

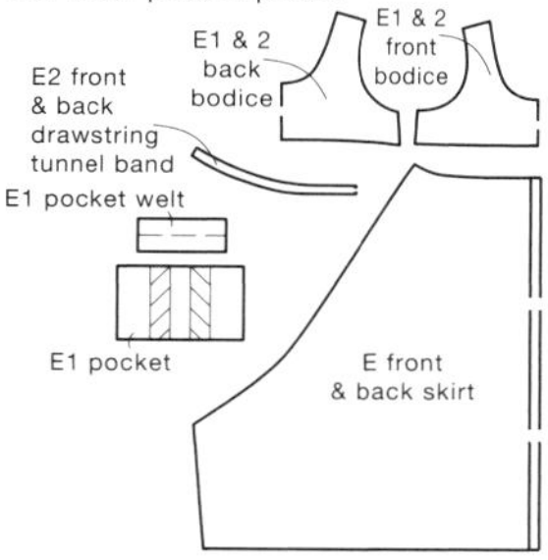

E1 & 2 back bodice
E1 & 2 front bodice
E2 front & back drawstring tunnel band
E1 pocket welt
E1 pocket
E front & back skirt

Finished measurements — Unit: in

		XS	S	M	L
Bust	E1, 2	36¼	38⅛	40⅛	42⅛
	E3	26		29⅛	
Center back length	E1, 2	35⅜			
	E3	43¼			

Finished measurements — Unit: cm

		XS	S	M	L
Bust	E1, 2	92	97	102	107
	E3	66		74	
Center back length	E1, 2	90			
	E3	110			

E1
p. 25 sundress

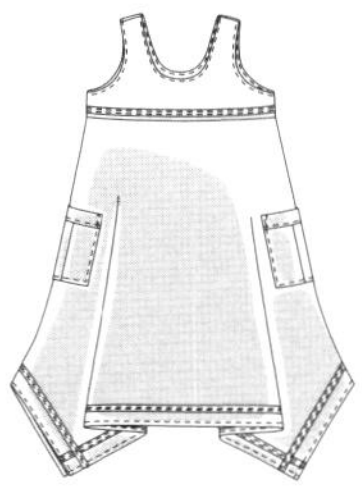

E2
p. 24 sundress

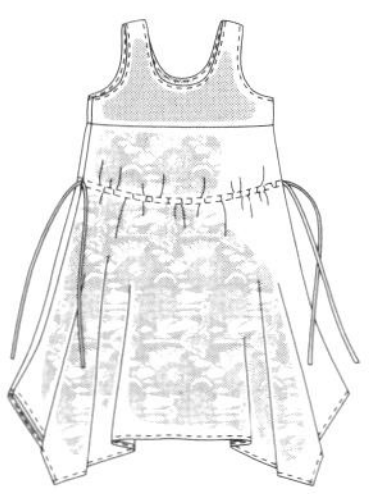

E3
p. 26 dress/skirt

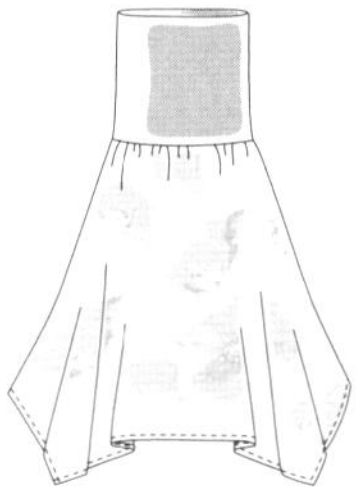

pattern F

A camisole dress with fairly wide shoulder straps. To provide a neat fit to the body, a length of elastic is passed through the top edge of the rectangle formed by the back bodice.
F1 is a midi-length dress with a generous number of gathers. F2, with fewer gathers than F1, is a box silhouette dress with four overlapping ruffles. F3 is shorter than F2 and has a single ruffle.

Full-scale pattern pieces

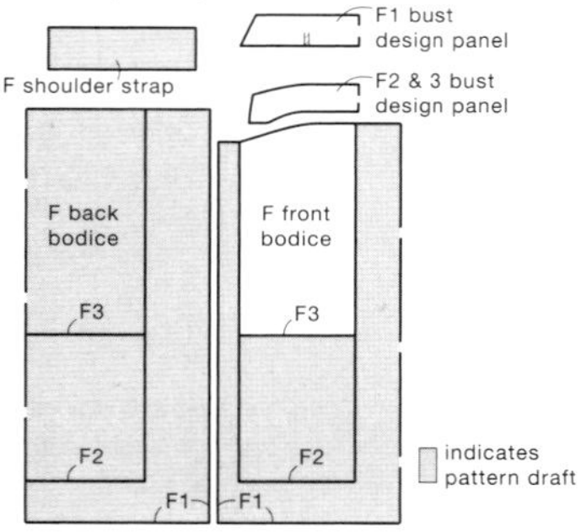

F1 bust design panel
F shoulder strap
F2 & 3 bust design panel
F back bodice
F front bodice
F3
F3
F2
F2
F1
F1
indicates pattern draft

Finished measurements — Unit: in

		XS	S	M	L
Bust		32⅝	34 7/16	36¼	37 15/16
Center back length	F1	39⅜			
	F2	34 13/16			
	F3	21 1/16			

Finished measurements — Unit: cm

		XS	S	M	L
Bust		83	87.5	92	96.5
Center back length	F1	100			
	F2	88.5			
	F3	53.5			

F1
p. 28 sundress

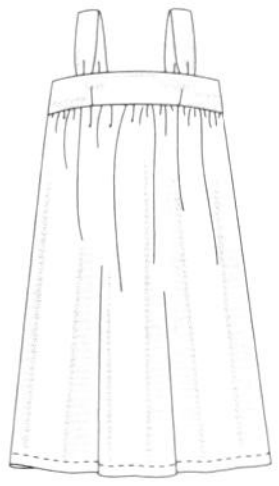

F2
p. 29 shift

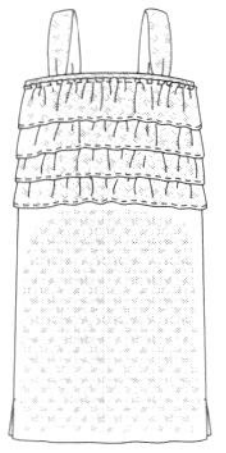

F3
p. 19 tunic

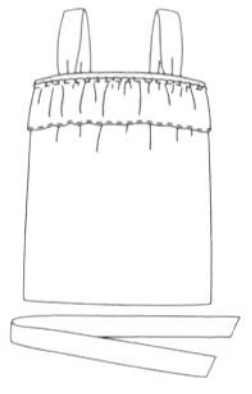

pattern G

A camisole dress with the same pattern piece for the front and back bodice. The top edge is threaded with elastic for a contoured fit to the body.
G1 is a full-length dress with bra top. G2 allows you to bring together a bare-shouldered dress and skirt. G3 uses the skirt as a tunic, with slim shoulder strap ties.

Full-scale pattern pieces

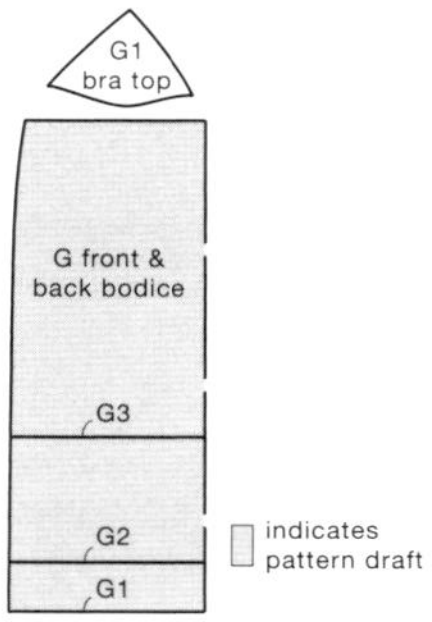

G1 bra top
G front & back bodice
G3
G2
G1
indicates pattern draft

Finished measurements — Unit: in

		XS	S	M	L
Bust		24¾	26¾	28¾	30¾
Center back length	G1	39⅜			
	G2	35⅜			
	G3	25⅝			

Finished measurements — Unit: cm

		XS	S	M	L
Bust		63	68	73	78
Center back length	G1	100			
	G2	90			
	G3	65			

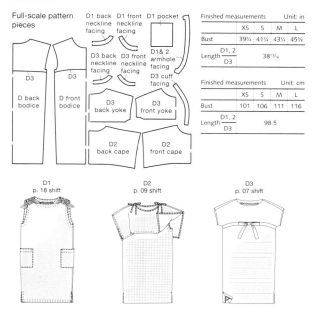

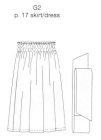

G1
p. 30 sundress

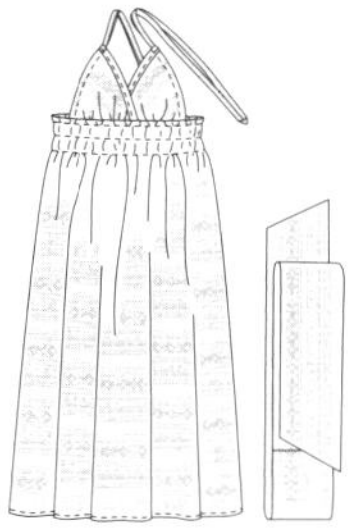

G2
p. 17 skirt/dress

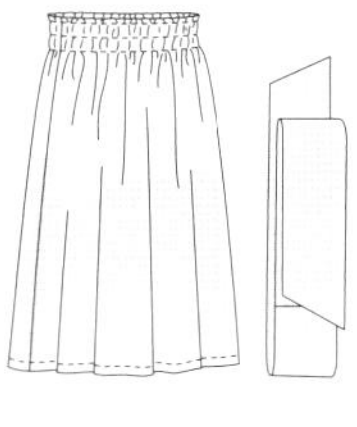

G3
p. 08 tunic

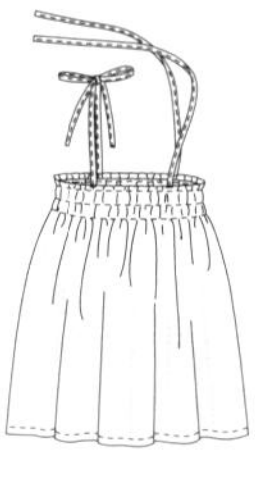

pattern A

A1

Dress ☛ page 06

A2

Tunic ☛ page 23

★ **Pattern pieces**

A front bodice **A** front side bodice **A** back bodice **A** back side bodice **A** front facing **A** back facing
Cut the ribbon and loop fabric to the measurements shown in the cutting layout.

★ **A1 materials**

Fabric (printed cotton lawn):
 XS/S—W 43¼ in x L 137¾ in (1.1 m x 3.5 m)
 M/L—W 43¼ in x L 145⅝ in (1.1 m x 3.7 m)
Fusible interfacing: W 35⅜ in x L 23⅝ in (90 cm x 60 cm)
Buttons: ¹⁵⁄₃₂ in (1.2 cm) diameter x 2

★ **A2 materials**

Fabric (silk seersucker):
 XS/S—W 42½ in x L 102⅜ in (1.08 m x 2.6 m)
 M/L—W 42½ in x L 106¼ in (1.08 m x 2.7 m)
Fusible interfacing: W 35⅜ in x L 23⅝ in (90 cm x 60 cm)
Buttons: ¹⁵⁄₃₂ in (1.2 cm) diameter x 2

★ **Sewing tips**

● The only difference between the tunic (**A2**) and the dress (**A1**) is the finishing of the hem. Otherwise, the instructions are the same for both.
● Attach the fusible interfacing to the wrong side of the facing, and then zigzag or overlock the bottom edge.

Cutting layout for A1 dress

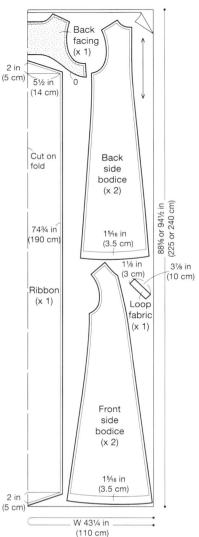

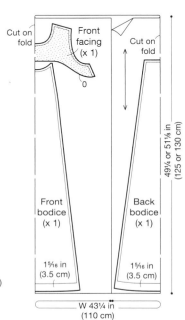

* Unless stipulated, the seam allowance is ⅜ in (1 cm)
* ▢ Attach the fusible interfacing here

Cutting layout for A2 tunic

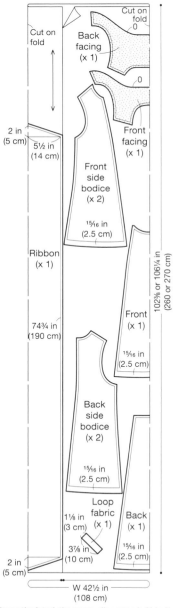

* Unless stipulated, the seam allowance is ⅜ in (1 cm)
* ▢ Attach the fusible interfacing here

Sewing sequence

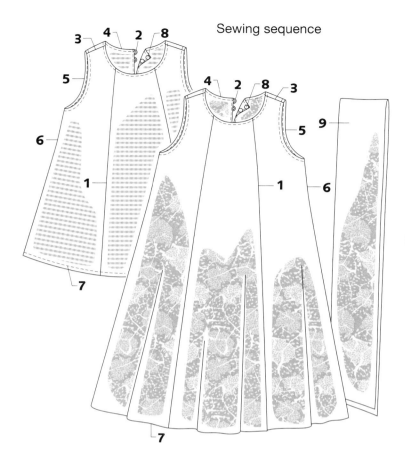

2 Make and baste on the loops

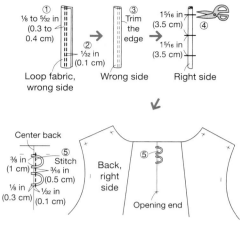

① Fold the loop fabric wrong side out and stitch ⅛ to ⁵⁄₃₂ in (0.3 to 0.4 cm) from the edge.
② Add another row of stitches along the edge.
③ Trim down to the narrow seam allowance along the edge of the stitching in ②.
④ Use a looper or other tool to turn the fabric right side out, and then cut two lengths of 1⁵⁄₁₆ in (3.5 cm).
⑤ Baste onto the right side of the center back bodice.

1 Sew the vertical seams

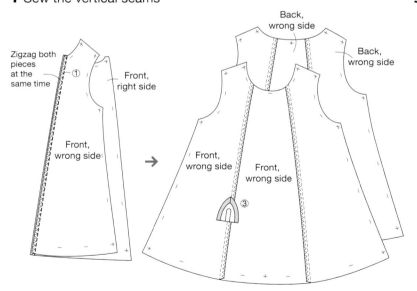

① Align the center bodice and side bodice (at both front and back) wrong side out and sew.
② Finish both seam allowances at the same time by zigzagging or overlocking.
③ Turn the seam allowances at both front and back into the center and iron them neatly in place.

3 Sew the shoulders

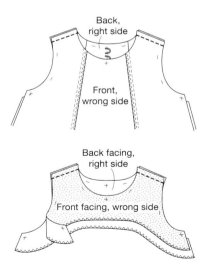

Sew the shoulders of the bodice and facing together, opening the seam allowance.

4 Sew the neckline

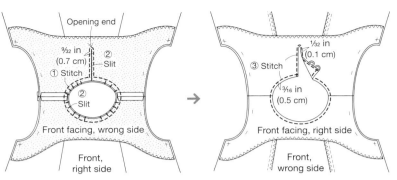

① Align the bodice and facing wrong side out and sew from the neckline to end of the opening in the back.

② Make a slash in the center back as far as the end of the opening. Make notches in the seam allowance of the neckline.

③ Turn the facing right side out and iron neatly in place, and then stitch the neckline and opening in the back.

5 Sew the armholes

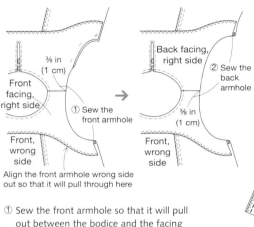

Align the front armhole wrong side out so that it will pull through here

① Sew the front armhole so that it will pull out between the bodice and the facing (which are turned right side out). Notch the seam allowance.

② Working in the same way, sew the back armhole, and then iron the entire armhole neatly into shape.

7 Finish the hem

● Dress

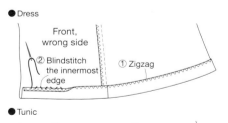

● Tunic

Front, wrong side

½2 to ³⁄₃₂ in (0.1 to 0.2 cm)

½ in (1.3 cm) triple fold

Zigzag the seam allowance of the hem of the dress, fold it up, and add a small amount of blindstitching to the innermost edge. For the hem of the tunic, stitch the seam allowance with a threefold hem.

6 Sew the sides

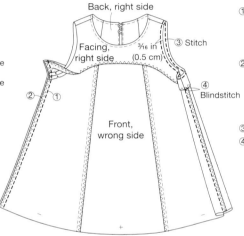

① Align the front and back sides wrong side out and sew as one seam as far as the facing.

② Zigzag the seam allowances on both pieces at the same time to finish them, and then turn the fabric to the back.

③ Stitch the armholes.

④ Blindstitch the bottom edge of the sides of the facing onto the seam allowance of the bodice.

8 Attach the buttons

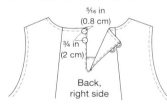

Attach the two buttons to the back left edge, ensuring that they are aligned with the positions of the loops on the right.

9 Sew the ribbon

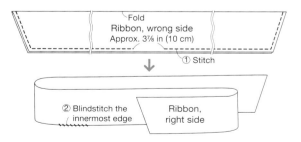

① Fold the ribbon wrong side out and sew, leaving an opening for turning out in the center.

② Turn the ribbon right side out and iron neatly before blindstitching the opening.

pattern A

A3

Dress ☛ page 10

★ Pattern pieces

A front bodice **A** front side bodice **A** back bodice **A** back side bodice **A** front facing **A** back facing **A3** ruffle
Cut the bias binding and loop fabric to the measurements shown in the cutting layout for fabric B.

★ Materials

Fabric A (polyester, big dot print):
  XS/S—W 43¼ in x L 90½ in (1.1 m x 2.3 m)
  M/L—W 43¼ in x L 98⅜ in (1.1 m x 2.5 m)
Fabric B (polyester, small dot print):
  W 43¼ in x L 43¼ in (1.1 m x 1.1 m)
Fusible interfacing: W 35⅜ in x L 23⅝ in (90 cm x 60 cm)
Buttons: ¹⁵⁄₃₂ in (1.2 cm) diameter x 2

★ For more detailed sewing instructions ▼, see pp. 37 and 38

- Attach the fusible interfacing to the wrong side of the facing, and zigzag or overlock the bottom edge.
1. Sew the ruffles and attach them to the front side bodice. → Figure page 40.
2. Sew the vertical seams at both front and back (▼), sandwiching the ruffles with the front seams.
3. Make and baste on the loops. ▼
4. Sew the shoulders. ▼
5. Make the opening in the back. → Figure page 40.
6. Hem the neckline. → Figure page 40.
7. Sew the armholes. ▼
8. Sew the sides together as far as the facing, and stitch the armholes. ▼
9. Blindstitch the hem. ▼
10. Attach the buttons. ▼

Sewing sequence

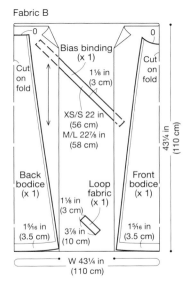

Cutting layout

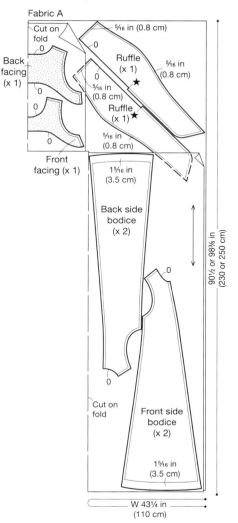

Fabric A

Back facing (x 1)

Ruffle (x 1)   ⁵⁄₁₆ in (0.8 cm)
⁵⁄₁₆ in (0.8 cm)
⁵⁄₁₆ in (0.8 cm)
Ruffle (x 1) ★
⁵⁄₁₆ in (0.8 cm)

Cut on fold

Front facing (x 1)

1⁵⁄₁₆ in (3.5 cm)

Back side bodice (x 2)

Cut on fold

Front side bodice (x 2)

1⁵⁄₁₆ in (3.5 cm)

90½ or 98⅜ in (230 or 250 cm)

W 43¼ in (110 cm)

* Unless stipulated, the seam allowance is ⅜ in (1 cm)
* ⬚ Attach the fusible interfacing here

Fabric B

Bias binding (x 1)   1⅛ in (3 cm)

Cut on fold

XS/S 22 in (56 cm)
M/L 22⅞ in (58 cm)

Cut on fold

Back bodice (x 1)

1⅛ in (3 cm)

Loop fabric (x 1)

3⅞ in (10 cm)

Front bodice (x 1)

1⁵⁄₁₆ in (3.5 cm)

1⁵⁄₁₆ in (3.5 cm)

43¼ in (110 cm)

W 43¼ in (110 cm)

1 Sew the ruffles and attach to the front side bodice

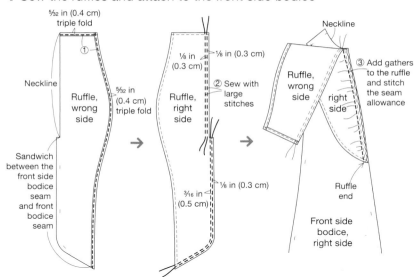

① Stitch the entire seam allowance of the ruffles with a threefold hem, except for the edges by which the ruffles will be attached to the bodice.

② Make two rows of large stitches on these edges, for gathers.

③ Pull the threads in the parts of the ruffles that are sandwiched between the front side bodice seam and the front bodice seam to create the gathers. Lay the ruffles over the seam allowance at the attachment position on the front side bodice, and then stitch or baste in place.

5 Make the opening in the back

① Align the back bodice and facing wrong side out and sew along the edge of where the opening is going to be located in the center back.

② Make a slit down the middle of the seam.

③ Turn the facing right side out and arrange neatly, then stitch along the opening.

④ Neatly arrange the neckline of the bodice and facing right side out and baste.

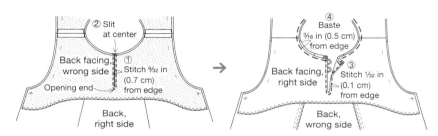

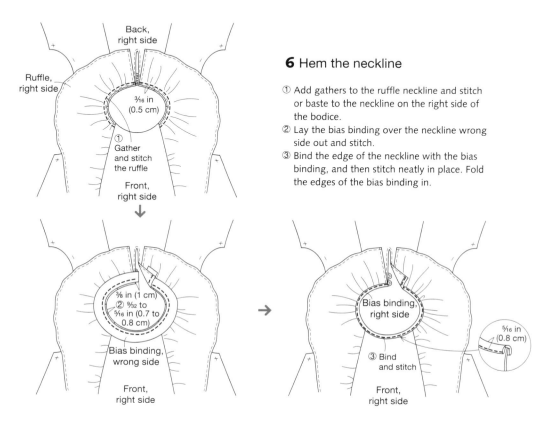

6 Hem the neckline

① Add gathers to the ruffle neckline and stitch or baste to the neckline on the right side of the bodice.

② Lay the bias binding over the neckline wrong side out and stitch.

③ Bind the edge of the neckline with the bias binding, and then stitch neatly in place. Fold the edges of the bias binding in.

pattern B

B1

Dress ☛ page 12

★ **Pattern pieces**
B front B back B sleeve **B1** collar **B1** gusset

★ **Materials**
Fabric (linen):
   XS/S—W 59 in x L 82⅝ in (1.5 m x 2.1 m)
   M/L—W 59 in x L 86⅝ in (1.5 m x 2.2 m)
Elastic: W ⁹⁄₁₆ in (1.5 cm), length to suit
Bias tape (double-fold):
   W ⁹⁄₁₆ in x L 82⅝ in (1.5 cm x 2.1 m)

★ **Sewing tip**
● Edge-stitch and finish the hem with ordinary bias tape. If you cannot find bias tape of the same color, make your own by cutting a bias 1⅛ in (3 cm) wide from the main fabric.

Cutting layout

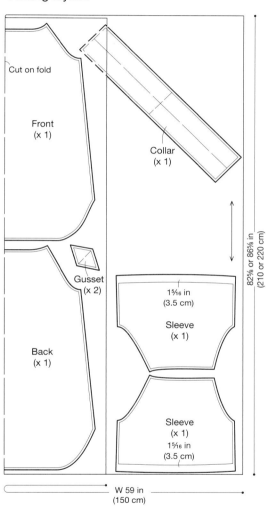

Cut on fold

Front
(x 1)

Collar
(x 1)

Gusset
(x 2)

Sleeve
(x 1)
1⁵⁄₁₆ in
(3.5 cm)

Back
(x 1)

Sleeve
(x 1)
1⁵⁄₁₆ in
(3.5 cm)

82⅝ or 86⅝ in
(210 or 220 cm)

W 59 in
(150 cm)

* Unless stipulated, the seam allowance is ⅜ in (1 cm)

Sewing sequence

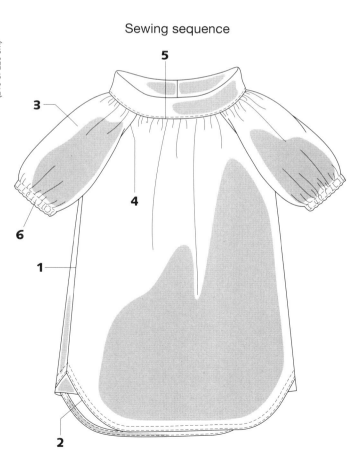

1 Sew the sides

① Align the front and back sides wrong side
   out and sew as far as the stitch end.
② Finish both seam allowances at the same time
   by zigzagging or overlocking them to around
   ⅜ in (1 cm) above the stitch end.
③ Turn the seam allowance toward the
   back and iron.

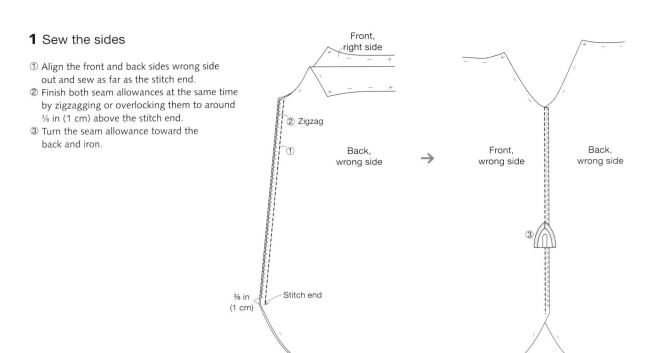

Front,
right side

② Zigzag

①

Back,
wrong side

⅜ in
(1 cm)

Stitch end

Front,
wrong side

Back,
wrong side

③

2 Attach the gusset and finish the hem

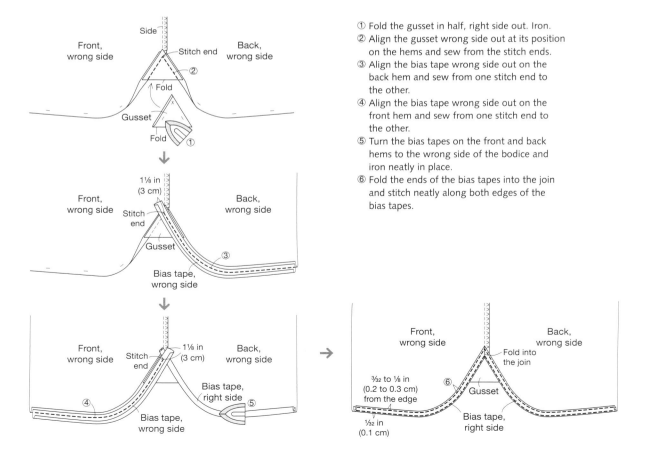

Side

Front,
wrong side

Stitch end

Back,
wrong side

②

Fold

Gusset

Fold ①

1⅛ in
(3 cm)

Front,
wrong side

Stitch
end

Back,
wrong side

Gusset

③

Bias tape,
wrong side

1⅛ in
(3 cm)

Front,
wrong side

Stitch
end

Back,
wrong side

Bias tape,
right side ⑤

④

Bias tape,
wrong side

① Fold the gusset in half, right side out. Iron.
② Align the gusset wrong side out at its position
   on the hems and sew from the stitch ends.
③ Align the bias tape wrong side out on the
   back hem and sew from one stitch end to
   the other.
④ Align the bias tape wrong side out on the
   front hem and sew from one stitch end to
   the other.
⑤ Turn the bias tapes on the front and back
   hems to the wrong side of the bodice and
   iron neatly in place.
⑥ Fold the ends of the bias tapes into the join
   and stitch neatly along both edges of the
   bias tapes.

Front,
wrong side

Back,
wrong side

Fold into
the join

⑥

Gusset

³⁄₃₂ to ⅛ in
(0.2 to 0.3 cm)
from the edge

¹⁄₃₂ in
(0.1 cm)

Bias tape,
right side

3 Sew the sleeves

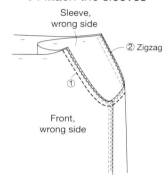

4 Attach the sleeves

③ Zigzag
①
② Slash the front seam allowance
³⁄₁₆ to ³⁄₈ in (0.5 to 1 cm)
¹⁵⁄₁₆ in (2.5 cm)
³⁄₈ in (1 cm)

Sleeve, wrong side

④
³⁄₃₂ to ¹⁄₈ in (0.2 to 0.3 cm)

Sleeve, wrong side
¹⁵⁄₁₆ in (2.5 cm)
³⁄₈ in (1 cm)
½₂ in (0.1 cm) ⑤ Opening for elastic

Sleeve, wrong side ② Zigzag
①
Front, wrong side

① Align the sleeve seams wrong side out and stitch them, leaving a ¹⁵⁄₁₆ in (2.5 cm) opening for the elastic on the seam allowance of the cuff.
② Add a slash to the front seam allowance of the sleeves between ³⁄₁₆ and ³⁄₈ in (0.5 and 1 cm) above the finishing line of the cuffs.
③ Finish both sleeve seam allowances at the same time by zigzagging them as far as the slash.

④ Fold the sleeve seam allowance toward the back, and then cut open and stitch the seam allowance from the slash down.
⑤ Fold the seam allowance of the cuff three times to a width of ¹⁵⁄₁₆ in (2.5 cm), stitching on both sides of the seam allowance.

① Align the bodice and sleeves wrong side out and sew the raglan lines to the front and back as one seam.
② Zigzag the seam allowances on both pieces of fabric at the same time to finish them, and then press them toward the sleeve.

5 Attach the collar

① Make two rows of large stitches on the seam allowance of the neckline, and then pull the thread to gather evenly.
② Sew the center back of the collar and open the seam allowance.
③ Iron a ³⁄₈ in (1 cm) fold on the seam allowance of the collar, wrong side out.
④ Align the collar with the neckline wrong side out and sew.
⑤ Fold the collar-end seam allowance toward the collar, folding the collar in half and stitching.

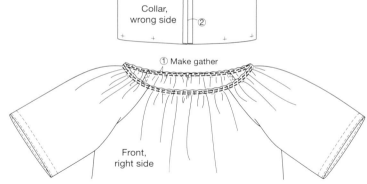

Collar, wrong side ②
① Make gather
Front, right side

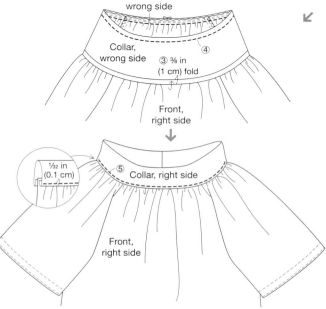

Back, wrong side
Collar, wrong side ④
③ ³⁄₈ in (1 cm) fold
Front, right side

½₂ in (0.1 cm) ⑤ Collar, right side
Front, right side

6 Pass the elastic through the cuffs

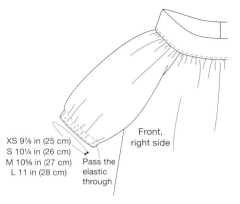

Front, right side

XS 9⅞ in (25 cm)
S 10¼ in (26 cm)
M 10⅝ in (27 cm)
L 11 in (28 cm)
Pass the elastic through

Cut the elastic ¾ in (2 cm) longer than indicated in the drawing and pass it through the cuff. Overlap the ends of the elastic by ¾ in (2 cm) and stitch in place.

B2

Lacy top ❦ page 15

★ Pattern pieces

B front **B** back **B** sleeve **B2** yoke **B2** front collar band **B2** back collar band

Cut the bias binding and loop fabric for finishing the opening in the back to the measurements shown in the cutting layout. Trace the pattern piece for the sleeve facing from the sleeve pattern piece.

★ Materials

Fabric (cotton seersucker):
  XS/S—W 40⅛ in x L 86⅝ in (1.02 m x 2.2 m)
  M/L—W 40⅛ in x L 90½ in (1.02 m x 2.3 m)
Sheer fusible interfacing:
  W 35⅜ in x L 7⅞ in (90 cm x 20 cm)
Lace A: W 2¹⁵⁄₁₆ in x L 59 in (7.5 cm x 1.5 m)
Lace B: W ⅜ in x L 173¼ in (1 cm x 4.4 m)
Elastic: W ⅜ in (1 cm), length to suit
Buttons: ¹³⁄₃₂ in (1.1 cm) diameter x 2

★ For more detailed sewing instructions ▼, see pp. 42 and 43

- Attach the fusible interfacing to the wrong side of the collar bands.
1. Make the opening in the center back. → page 46.
2. Attach the yoke and lace A to the front bodice. → Figure page 45.
3. Sew the sides. ▼
4. Stitch the hem with a ⁵⁄₁₆ in (0.8 cm) wide threefold hem.
5. Sew the sleeves. → Figure page 45.
6. Attach the sleeves. ▼
7. Make the loops and baste them to the back collar band. → Figure page 45.
8. Add gathers to the sleeves and back bodice neckline, and then attach the collar bands. → page 47.
9. Attach lace B around the full circumference of the collar bands, leaving the back opening free. Attach the lace on both left and right ⁹⁄₁₆ in (1.5 cm) in from the center front, leaving a 31½ (80 cm) length in the ribbons from that point.
10. Pass the elastic through the cuffs. The finished length of the elastic is: XS 8⅝ in (22 cm), S 9 in (23 cm), M 9½ in (24 cm), and L 9⅞ in (25 cm). ▼
11. Attach the buttons.

Cutting layout

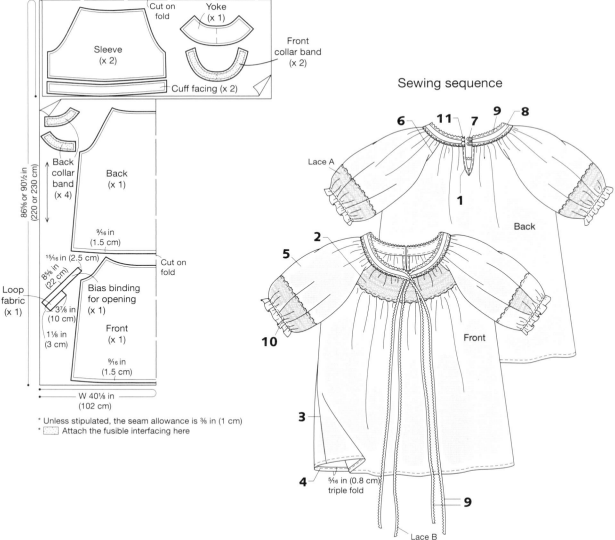

Sleeve (x 2)
Cut on fold
Yoke (x 1)
Front collar band (x 2)
Cuff facing (x 2)

86⅝ or 90½ in (220 or 230 cm)

Back collar band (x 4)
Back (x 1)
⁹⁄₁₆ in (1.5 cm)
1⁵⁄₁₆ in (2.5 cm)
Cut on fold

Loop fabric (x 1)
8⅝ in (22 cm)
Bias binding for opening (x 1)
Front (x 1)
3⅞ in (10 cm)
1⅛ in (3 cm)
⁹⁄₁₆ in (1.5 cm)

W 40⅛ in (102 cm)

* Unless stipulated, the seam allowance is ⅜ in (1 cm)
* ▨ Attach the fusible interfacing here

Sewing sequence

Lace A
Back
Front
1
2
3
4 ⁵⁄₁₆ in (0.8 cm) triple fold
5
6 11 7 9 8
9
10
Lace B

2 Attach the yoke and lace A to the front

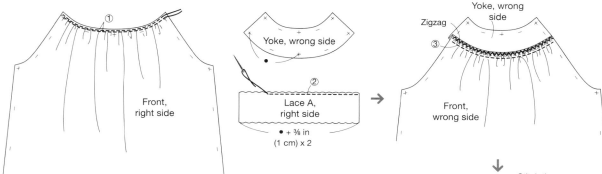

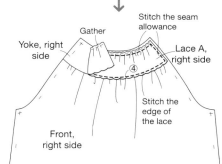

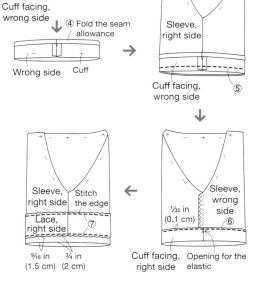

① Make two rows of large stitches on the seam allowance of the top edge of the front piece, and then pull the threads to make the gathers.

② Cut lace A to the same length as the yoke and sew with a fairly large running stitch along the top edge.

③ Align the front and yoke wrong side out and sew together. Zigzag the seam allowances on both pieces of fabric at the same time to finish them, and then fold them toward the yoke.

④ Pull the thread with which you running-stitched the lace, bringing the fabric in to match the neckline measurement of the yoke. Lay the lace over the right side of the yoke and stitch around the edge.

5 Sew the sleeves

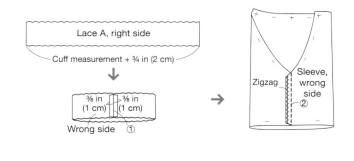

① Cut lace A to match the cuff size, then sew the two ends together wrong side out to form a loop.

② Sew the sleeve seams, zigzag the seam allowances on both pieces of fabric at the same time to finish them, and then turn them to the back.

③ Sew the sleeve seams of the cuff facings, leaving an opening for the elastic, and open the seam allowance.

④ Fold in the seam allowance at the top edge of the cuff facings with an iron.

⑤ Align the sleeves and the facings wrong side out and sew the cuffs.

⑥ Turn the cuff facings to the wrong side of the sleeves and set neatly in place, then stitch the edge of the facings.

⑦ Lay the lace sewn into a loop over the right side of the sleeves and stitch both ends of the lace.

7 Make the loops and baste them to the back collar band

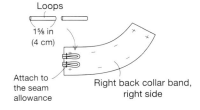

Make two loops (→ page 37) and baste them into position on the right side of the right back collar band.

pattern B

B3

Blouse ➤ page 04

★ Pattern pieces

B front **B** back **B** sleeve **B3** front collar band **B3** back collar band

Cut the bias binding for finishing the opening in the front to the measurements shown in the cutting layout. Trace the pattern pieces for the reinforcement band from the back pattern piece.

★ Materials

Fabric (cotton print):
  XS/S—W 41⅜ in x L 86⅝ in (1.05 m x 2.2 m)
  M/L—W 41⅜ in x L 90½ in (1.05 m x 2.3 m)
Fusible interfacing: W 35⅜ in x L 7⅞ in (90 cm x 20 cm)
Lace: W ⅜ in x L 110¼ in (1 cm x 2.8 m)
Elastic: W ⅜ in (1 cm), length to suit

★ For more detailed sewing instructions ▼, see pp. 42 and 43

- Attach the fusible interfacing to the wrong side of the collar band.
1. Make the opening in the center front. → Figure below.
2. Sew the sides. ▼
3. Attach the reinforcement band for the drawstring tunnel to the back fabric piece and the lace to the hem. → Figure page 47.
4. Sew the sleeves. First sew the sleeve seams, zigzag or overlock the seam allowances on both pieces of fabric at the same time to finish them, and then turn them to the back. Working in the same way as you did with the hem, now attach the lace to the cuffs.
5. Attach the sleeves. ▼
6. Sew the collar bands. → Figure page 47.
7. Attach the collar bands. → Figure page 47.
8. Pass the elastic through the reinforcement band. The finished length of the elastic is: XS 30¾ in (78 cm), S 32⅝ in (83 cm), M 34⅝ in (88 cm), and L 36⅝ in (93 cm). ▼

Cutting layout

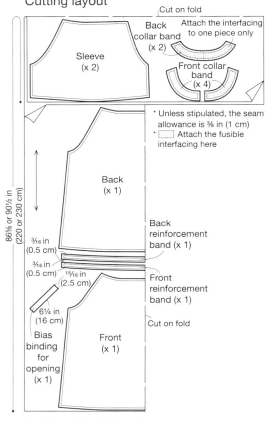

Sewing sequence

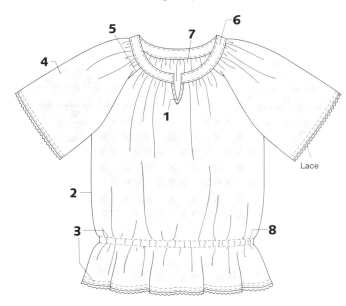

1 Make the opening in the center front

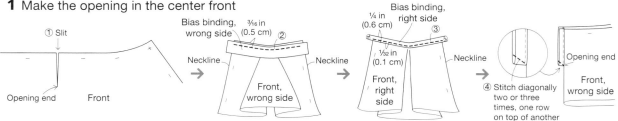

① Make a slit in the center front as far as the end of the opening.

② Open out the slit, align the right side of the bias binding with the right side of the opening, and stitch.

③ Bind the edge of the back opening with the bias binding, then fold into a width of ¼ in (0.6 cm) and stitch. Trim off any fabric that protrudes from the neckline.

④ Align the opening wrong side out and stitch the binding at the end of the opening diagonally.

3 Attach the reinforcement band to the back and the lace to the hem

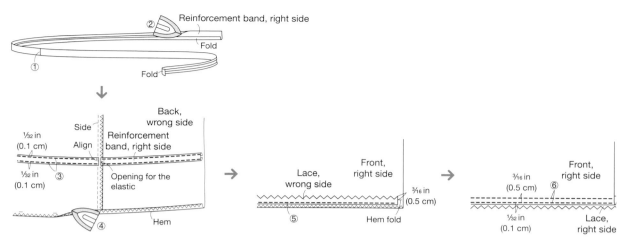

① Sew the front and back reinforcement bands together at one end.
② Fold down the seam allowance around the reinforcement band with an iron.

③ Attach the reinforcement band at the appropriate position on the wrong side of the back fabric piece and stitch the ends on either side.
④ Zigzag the seam allowance of the hem on the front and back pieces and then fold in the seam allowance with an iron.

⑤ Align the lace with the fold in the hem wrong side out as shown in the drawing, and stitch the edge of the lace onto the seam allowance.
⑥ Fold the hem down and stitch in two rows.

6 Sew the collar bands

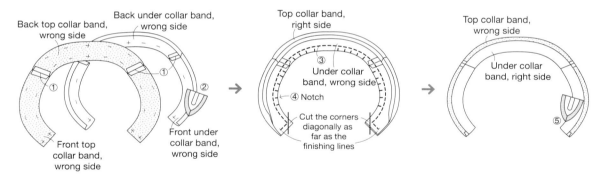

① Using the collar band to which you have attached the fusible interfacing as the top band, sew the sections of the top and under collar bands together.

② Fold the seam allowance around the outside of the under collar band with an iron.
③ Align the top and under collar bands wrong side out and sew the front edge and neckline.

④ Notch the seam allowance of the neckline. Cut the seam allowance on the corners of the front edge diagonally.
⑤ Turn the collar band to the right side and iron neatly in place.

7 Attach the collar bands

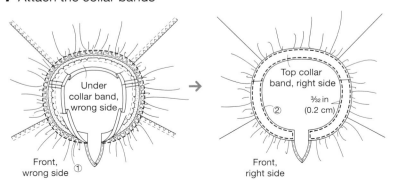

① Gather the neckline of the blouse and align it wrong side out with the top collar band. Turn the seam allowance toward the collar band and set neatly in place.
② Arrange the top and under collar bands right side out, and stitch around the outside edge of the collar bands.

pattern C

C1

Dress 🦋 page 20

★ Pattern pieces

C front bodice **C** back bodice **C1** sleeve **C** front facing **C** back facing

Cut the reinforcement band for the ribbon opening to the measurements shown in the cutting layout for the lightweight cotton facing. Trace the pattern piece for the sleeve facing from the sleeve pattern piece.

★ Materials

Fabric (linen with eyelet lace edging):
XS/S—W 55⅛ in x L 82⅝ in (1.4 m x 2.1 m)
M/L—W 55⅛ in x L 86⅝ in (1.4 m x 2.2 m)
Facing (lightweight cotton):
W 29½ in x L 7⅞ in (75 cm x 20 cm)
Lightweight fusible interfacing:
W 35⅜ in x L 9⅞ in (90 cm x 25 cm)
Grosgrain ribbon: W ¹⁵⁄₁₆ in x L 94½ in (2.5 cm x 2.4 m)

★ Sewing tips

● The design uses fabric with a scalloped lace selvage, meaning that the scallop can be used for the hem with no need for further modification. For this reason, the hem line on the pattern piece is shown as a straight line. If you are working with standard fabric, use the hem line shown in C3, adding a seam allowance before cutting the fabric and blindstitching the hem.

● Attach the fusible interfacing to the wrong side of both the front and back facing and the reinforcement bands for the ribbon.

Cutting layout

Fabric
* When you cut the sleeves, lay them out flat (opening the fold)

Sleeve (x 1)
0
Front facing (x 1)
Cut on fold
Scalloped
Front bodice (x 1)

Back facing (x 1)
0
Sleeve (x 1)
Back bodice (x 1)
Scalloped
Cut on fold

82⅝ or 86⅝ in (210 or 220 cm)

W 55⅛ in (140 cm)

Lightweight cotton facing
Fold
Cuff facing (x 2)
1⅛ in (3 cm)
7⅞ in (20cm)
1¹³⁄₁₆ in (4.5 cm)
29½ in (75 cm)
Reinforcement band for ribbon tunnel (x 4)

* Unless stipulated, the seam allowance is ⅜ in (1 cm)
* ▢ Attach the fusible interfacing here

Sewing sequence

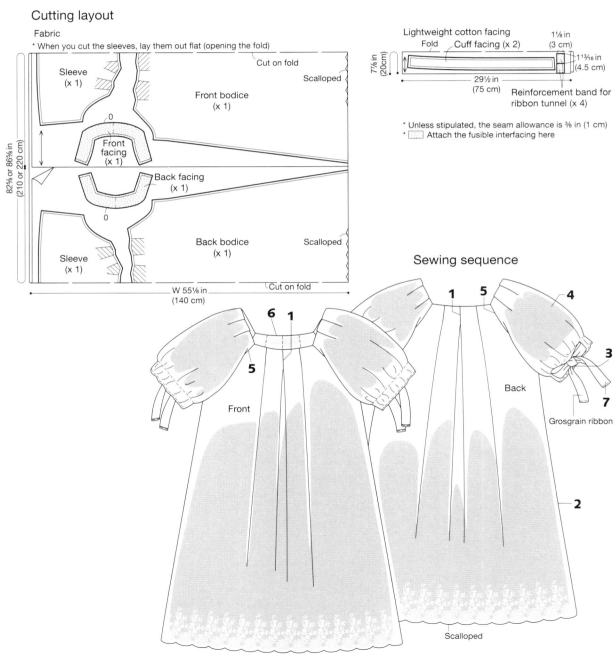

Front

Back

Grosgrain ribbon

Scalloped

1 Sew the tucks in the bodice

① Pinch the tucks wrong side out, sewing as far as the stitch end.
② Cut open the middle tuck and turn the side tucks out to the sides, ironing concealed pleats in each of them to around 3⅞ in (10 cm) from the neckline.
③ Stitch the seam allowance on the neckline to secure the tucks in place.

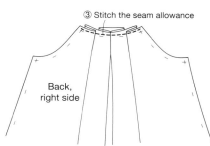

2 Sew the sides

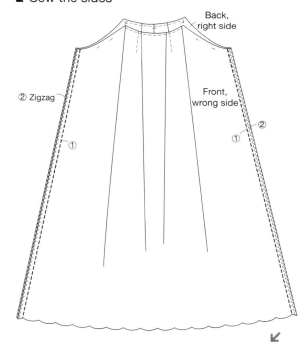

① Align the front and back sides wrong side out and sew.
② Finish both seam allowances at the same time by zigzagging or overlocking.
③ Turn the seam allowance toward the back and iron neatly in place, stitching only the hem of the seam allowance.

3 Make the tunnel for the ribbon in the cuffs

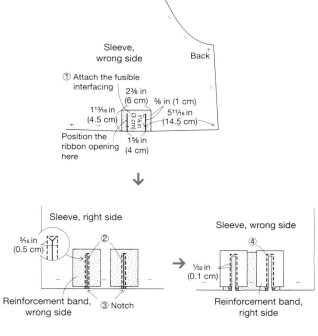

① Attach fusible interfacing to the back of the cuffs in the position shown, marking two openings for the ribbon to go through.
② Align the reinforcement band (wrong side out) with the tunnel opening and stitch ³⁄₁₆ in (0.5 cm) from the edge.
③ Make a notch down the middle of the seam.
④ Push the reinforcement band through the opening to the wrong side of the sleeve, iron neatly in place, and stitch.

4 Fold the tucks and make the sleeves

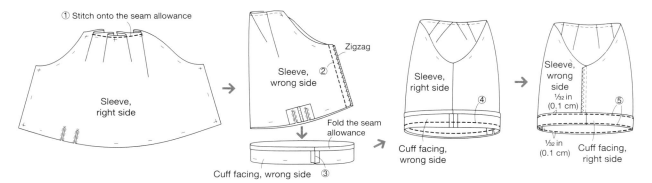

① Stitch onto the seam allowance

Sleeve, right side

Zigzag

Sleeve, ② wrong side

Fold the seam allowance

Cuff facing, wrong side ③

Sleeve, right side

④

Cuff facing, wrong side

Sleeve, wrong side

1/32 in (0.1 cm)

⑤

1/32 in (0.1 cm)   Cuff facing, right side

① Fold the tucks in the sleeve caps and stitch along the seam allowance.
② Align the sleeve seams wrong side out and sew. Zigzag the seam allowances on both pieces of fabric at the same time to finish them, and then turn them toward the back.

③ Sew the sleeve seams of the cuff facings and fold the top seam allowance with an iron.
④ Align the sleeves and facings wrong side out and sew the cuffs.
⑤ Turn the facings to the wrong side of the sleeves and set neatly in place before stitching.

5 Attach the sleeves

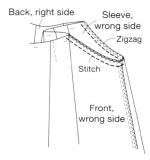

Back, right side   Sleeve, wrong side

Zigzag

Stitch

Front, wrong side

Align the dress and sleeves wrong side out and sew the raglan seams to the front and back. Zigzag the seam allowances on both pieces of fabric at the same time to finish them, and then fold them toward the sleeves.

7 Pass the ribbon through the cuffs

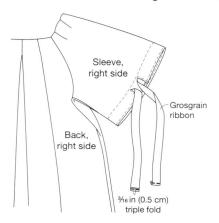

Sleeve, right side

Grosgrain ribbon

Back, right side

3/16 in (0.5 cm) triple fold

Cut a 47¼ in (1.2 m) length of grosgrain ribbon, stitch the ends with a threefold hem, and pass the ribbon through the openings in the cuffs.

6 Sew the neckline

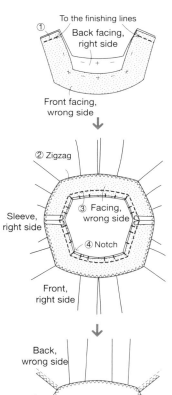

① To the finishing lines

Back facing, right side

Front facing, wrong side

② Zigzag

③ Facing, wrong side

Sleeve, right side

④ Notch

Front, right side

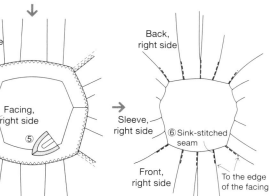

Back, wrong side

Facing, right side

⑤

Front, wrong side

Back, right side

Sleeve, right side

⑥ Sink-stitched seam

Front, right side

To the edge of the facing

① Sew the shoulders of the front and back neckline facing together, opening the seam allowance.
② Zigzag around the edge of the neckline facing.
③ Align the facing (wrong side out) with the neckline of the dress and sew.
④ Notch the seam allowance of the neckline. Notch the corners as far as the seam.
⑤ Turn the facing right side out and iron the neckline neatly in place.
⑥ Working from the right side of the bodice, sink-stitch the seams of the tucks and sleeve ends to secure the facing.

pattern C

C2

Blouse ❧ page 14

★ **Pattern pieces**

C front bodice C back bodice C2 sleeve C front facing C back facing

Cut the armhole bias binding to the measurements shown in the cutting layout.

★ **Materials**

Fabric (silk shantung):
XS/S—W 43¼ in x L 66⅞ in (1.1 m x 1.7 m)
M/L—W 43¼ in x L 70⅞ in (1.1 m x 1.8 m)
Sheer fusible interfacing:
W 35⅜ in x L 9⅞ in (90 cm x 25 cm)

★ **For more detailed sewing instructions ▼, see pp. 49 and 50**

- Attach the fusible interfacing to the wrong side of the facing. ▼
1. Sew the tucks in the bodice. ▼
2. Sew the sides. ▼
3. Stitch the hem with a ⁹⁄₁₆ in (1.5 cm) wide threefold hem.
4. Make the sleeves. → Figure below.
5. Attach the sleeves. Align the bodice and raglan seams of the sleeves wrong side out and sew as far as the sleeve ends (both front and back). Finish both seam allowances at the same time by zigzagging or overlocking and turn toward the bodice.
6. Finish the armholes. Edge-stitch the armholes, from the sleeve ends of the bodice down, with the bias binding, and then stitch on.
7. Sew the neckline. ▼

Cutting layout

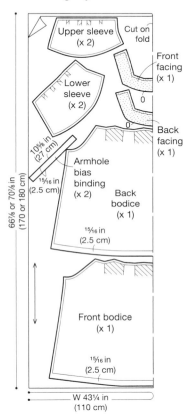

* Unless stipulated, the seam allowance is ⅜ in (1 cm)
* ▨ Attach the fusible interfacing here

Sewing sequence

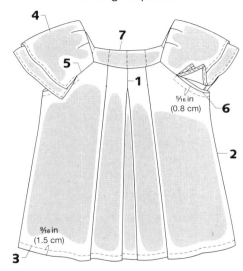

4 Make the sleeves

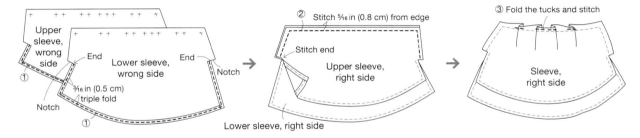

① Add notches to the seam allowance at the ends of the upper and lower sleeves, then stitch the lower hem below the notches in a threefold hem and finish by stitching the sides.

② Overlaying the upper and lower sleeves, stitch the seam allowance from above the stitch ends to secure both layers of fabric in place.

③ Fold the tucks in both sleeve caps at the same time, stitching or basting in place.

pattern C
C3
Dress ➜ page 32

★ **Pattern pieces**
C front bodice **C** back bodice **C3** sleeve **C3** bow knot bodice panel **C** front facing **C** back facing
Cut the center piece for the bow knot to the measurements shown in the cutting layout.

★ **Materials**
Fabric (linen stripe):
   XS/S—W 59 in x L 90½ in (1.5 m x 2.3 m)
   M/L—W 59 in x L 94½ in (1.5 m x 2.4 m)
Sheer fusible interfacing:
   W 35⅜ in x L 9⅞ in (90 cm x 25 cm)
Elastic: W ⅜ in (1 cm), length to suit

★ **For more detailed sewing instructions ▼, see pp. 49 and 50**

● Attach the fusible interfacing to the wrong side of the facing.
1. Sew the tucks in the bodice. ▼
2. Make the bow knot bodice panel and attach it to the front bodice. → Figure below.
3. Sew the sides. ▼
4. Make the sleeves. First fold the tucks in the sleeve caps and sew the sleeve seams ▼. Next, make a 9⁄16 (1.5 cm) wide threefold hem on the cuffs and stitch, leaving a tunnel around the cuffs for the elastic to go through.
5. Attach the sleeves. ▼
6. Sew the neckline. ▼
7. Zigzag the seam allowance of the hem, fold to the finishing seam and blindstitch.
8. Pass the elastic through the cuffs. The finished length of the elastic is: XS 11⅜ in (29 cm), S 11¾ in (30 cm), M 12¼ in (31 cm), and L 12⅝ in (32 cm).

Cutting layout

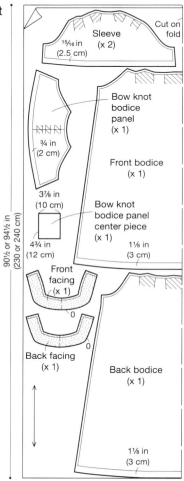

Sleeve (x 2)
Cut on fold
15⁄16 in (2.5 cm)
Bow knot bodice panel (x 1)
¾ in (2 cm)
Front bodice (x 1)
3⅞ in (10 cm)
Bow knot bodice panel center piece (x 1)
4¾ in (12 cm)
1⅛ in (3 cm)
Front facing (x 1)
0
Back facing (x 1)
0
Back bodice (x 1)
1⅛ in (3 cm)
90½ or 94½ in (230 or 240 cm)

* Unless stipulated, the seam allowance is ⅜ in (1 cm)
* ▦ Attach the fusible interfacing here

Sewing sequence

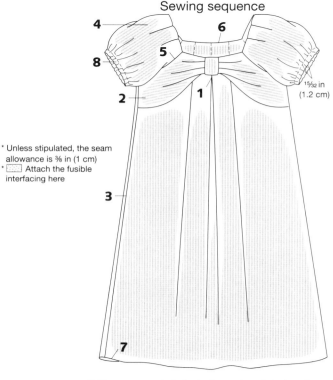

4   6
5
8
15⁄32 in (1.2 cm)
2   1
3
7

① Zigzag or overlock the bottom edge of the bow knot bodice panel.
② Pinch the tucks in the bow knot bodice panel (wrong side out), sew from one stitch end to the other, and then turn the tucks toward the top.
③ Fold and blindstitch the seam allowance on the bottom edge of the bow knot bodice panel.
④ Fold the center piece for the bow knot wrong side out and open the seam allowance.
⑤ Turn the center piece right side out and set neatly in place with the seam in the middle.
⑥ Align the middle of the center piece with the center front of the front bodice (right side up) and stitch onto the seam allowance of the neckline.
⑦ Overlay the bow knot bodice panel, fold the center piece up, and stitch or baste the seam allowance around the edge.
⑧ Fold up the knot and blindstitch in place.

2 Make the bow knot bodice panel and attach it to the front bodice

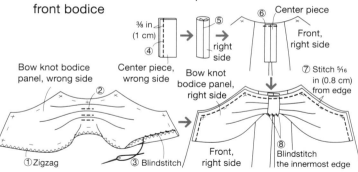

⅜ in (1 cm)
④
Center piece, wrong side
⑤
Center piece
⑥
right side
Front, right side
⑦ Stitch 5⁄16 in (0.8 cm) from edge
Bow knot bodice panel, wrong side
②
Bow knot bodice panel, right side
Front, right side
⑧ Blindstitch the innermost edge
① Zigzag
③ Blindstitch

D1

Shift ❧ page 18

★ Pattern pieces
D front bodice **D** back bodice **D1** front neckline facing
D1 back neckline facing **D1** armhole facing **D1** pocket

★ Materials
Fabric (linen):
  XS/S—W 55⅛ in x L 59 in (1.4 m x 1.5 m)
  M/L—W 55⅛ in x L 63 in (1.4 m x 1.6 m)
Fusible interfacing: W 35⅜ in x L 21⅝ in (90 cm x 55 cm)
Elastic: W 5/16 in (0.8 cm), length to suit
Grosgrain ribbon:
  W 2 in x L 39⅜ to 43¼ in (5 cm x 1 to 1.1 m)

★ Sewing tip
● Pass the elastic through the shoulders and gather them before tying decorative bows in the grosgrain ribbon for a finishing flourish.

Cutting layout

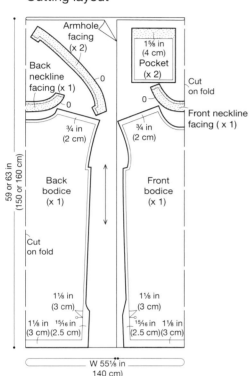

* Unless stipulated, the seam allowance is ⅜ in (1 cm)
* ░ Attach the fusible interfacing here

Sewing sequence

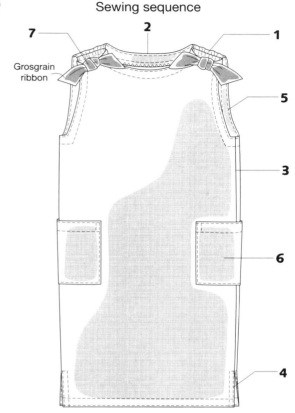

How to attach the fusible interfacing and finish the seam allowance

Attach the fusible interfacing to the wrong side of the facings and pocket welt seam allowances, and then zigzag or overlock the seam allowance at the positions shown in the drawing below.

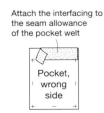

Attach the interfacing to the seam allowance of the pocket welt

Pocket, wrong side

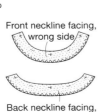

Front neckline facing, wrong side

Back neckline facing, wrong side

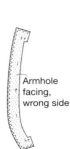

Armhole facing, wrong side

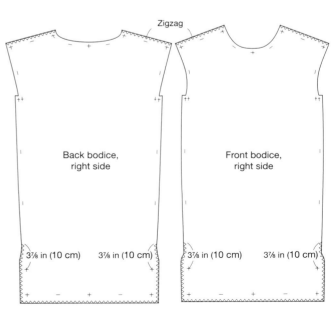

Zigzag

Back bodice, right side

Front bodice, right side

3⅞ in (10 cm)   3⅞ in (10 cm)

3⅞ in (10 cm)   3⅞ in (10 cm)

1 Sew the shoulders and pass the elastic through

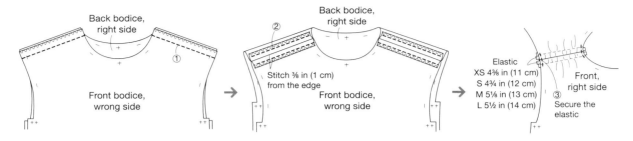

① Align the shoulders of the front and back bodices wrong side out and sew.
② Open the seam allowance and stitch both sides of the seam.

③ Pass the elastic between the shoulder seam and the stitching at the front and back, and then attach both ends of the elastic to the seam allowances.

2 Sew the neckline

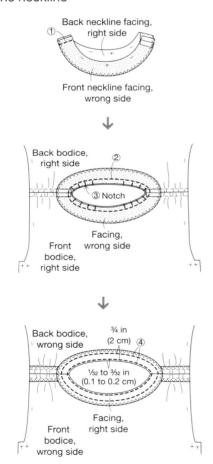

① Sew the shoulders of the front and back neckline facings, opening the seam allowance.
② Align the bodice and facing wrong side out and sew the neckline.
③ Notch the seam allowance of the neckline.
④ Turn the facing onto the wrong side of the bodice, iron neatly in place, and stitch in two rows.

3 Sew the sides

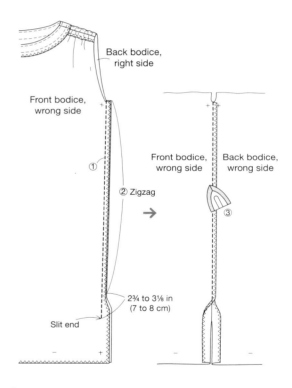

① Align the sides of the front and back bodices wrong side out and sew as far as the slit end.
② Finish both seam allowances at the same time by zigzagging them to between 2¾ and 3⅛ in (7 and 8 cm) above the slit end.
③ Turn the side seam allowance toward the back. Open the seam allowance of the slit opening.

4 Finish the hem and slit

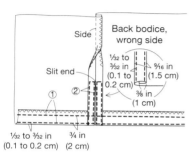

① Fold the hem to the finishing line with an iron, stitching in two rows.
② Make a 9/16 in (1.5 cm) wide threefold hem on the seam allowance of the slit, stitching in two rows.

5 Sew the armholes

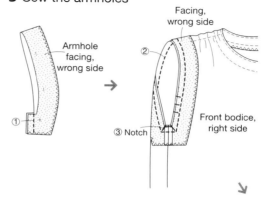

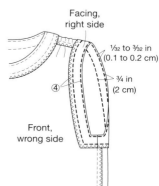

① Align the sides of the armhole facings wrong side out and sew. Open the seam allowance.
② Align the facing (wrong side out) with the bodice armholes and sew.
③ Notch the corners of the armholes and the seam allowance in the curved section. Notch the corners as far as the seam.
④ Turn the facing onto the wrong side of the bodice, iron neatly in place, and stitch in two rows.

6 Attach the pockets

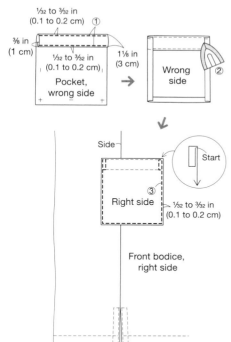

① Stitch the welts with a threefold hem.
② Fold the seam allowance around the pockets with an iron.
③ Sew the pockets onto the bodice at the attachment positions. Make a rectangle of stitches at both corners of the welt.

7 Tie ribbon bows to the shoulders

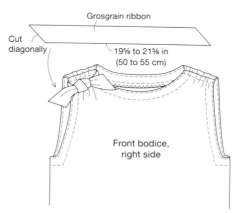

Make a 19⅝ to 21⅝ in (50 to 55 cm) length of grosgrain ribbon into a bow, and tie around one shoulder. Repeat on the other shoulder.

pattern D

D2

Shift ➤ page 09

★ Pattern pieces

D front bodice **D** back bodice **D2** front cape
D2 back cape **D2** armhole facing
Cut the bias binding and drawstring to the measurements shown in the cutting layout.

★ Materials

Fabric (two-ply cotton gauze):
  XS/S—W 44⅛ in x L 118⅛ in (1.12 m x 3 m)
  M/L—W 44⅛ in x L 122 in (1.12 m x 3.1 m)
Fusible interfacing:
  W 35⅜ in x L 19⅝ in (90 cm x 50 cm)
Fusible stay tape (half-bias):
  W ⅜ in x L 27⅝ in (1 cm x 70 cm)

★ Sewing tip

● This design uses a double-faced fabric, in the form of a large check (for the front and back bodice and armhole facings) and a smaller check (for the front and back capes, drawstring, and bias binding).

★ For more detailed sewing instructions ▼, see pp. 53 to 55

● Attach the fusible stay tape to the neckline on the front and back bodices, and the fusible interfacing to the wrong side of the armhole facing. Zigzag or overlock the hem, the slit opening of the bodice, the outside edge of the armhole facings (▼), and the shoulder seam allowances of the cape.

1 Sew the shoulders of the bodice. Zigzag the seam allowances on both pieces of fabric at the same time to finish them, and then turn them toward the back.
2 Sew the sides. ▼
3 Finish the hem and slit. → Figure page 57.
4 Sew the armholes. ▼
5 Sew the cape. → Figure page 57.
6 Lay the cape over the bodice and hem the neckline. → Figure page 57.
7 Make the drawstring and stitch onto the shoulders. → Figure page 57.

Cutting layout

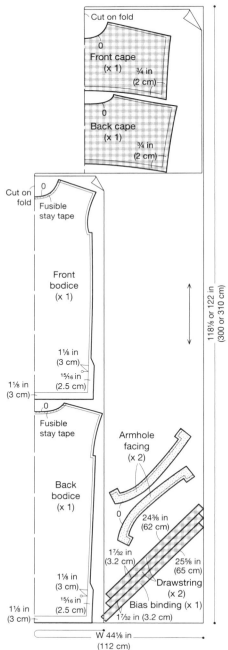

Sewing sequence

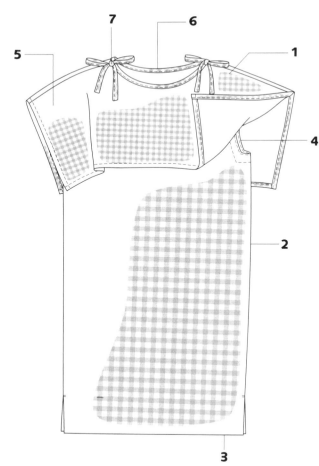

* Unless stipulated, the seam allowance is ⅜ in (1 cm)
* ▨ Attach the fusible interfacing here
* ▨ Use the side with the smaller check as the right side

3 Finish the hem and slit

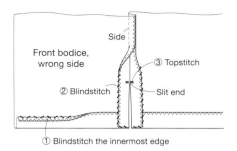

① Blindstitch the innermost edge

Front bodice, wrong side
Side
③ Topstitch
② Blindstitch
Slit end

① Fold up the hem with an iron and blindstitch just inside the edge of the hem.
② Blindstitch the edge of the seam allowance of the slit.
③ Topstitch the slit end two or three times, one row on top of the other.

5 Sew the cape

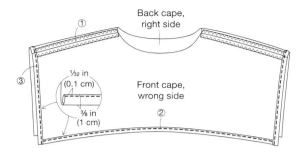

Back cape, right side
①
③
1/32 in (0.1 cm)
3/8 in (1 cm)
Front cape, wrong side
②

① Sew together the front and back shoulders and open the seam allowance.
② Stitch the bottom edge of the front and back capes with a 3/8 in (1 cm) wide threefold hem.
③ Stitch the sides with a 3/8 in (1 cm) wide threefold hem.

6 Lay the cape over the bodice and hem the neckline

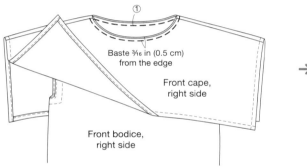

①
Baste 3/16 in (0.5 cm) from the edge
Front cape, right side
Front bodice, right side

→

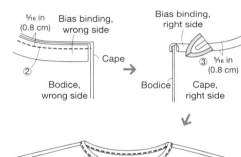

5/16 in (0.8 cm)
Bias binding, wrong side
②
Cape
Bodice, wrong side

→

Bias binding, right side
③ 5/16 in (0.8 cm)
Bodice
Cape, right side

↓

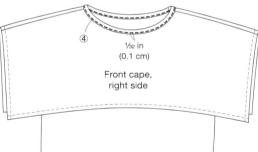

④
1/32 in (0.1 cm)
Front cape, right side

① Lay the cape over the bodice and baste onto the neckline.
② Align the bias binding with the wrong side of the bodice neckline and stitch.
③ Bind the edge with the bias binding, fold into a width of 5/16 in (0.8 cm), and then iron.
④ Topstitch along the edge of the bias binding, working with the cape right side out. Blindstitch the end of the binding.

7 Make the drawstring and stitch onto the shoulders

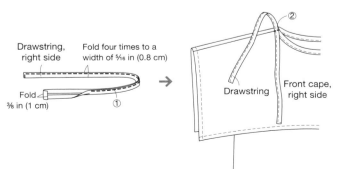

Drawstring, right side
Fold four times to a width of 5/16 in (0.8 cm)
Fold 3/8 in (1 cm)
①

→

Drawstring
②
Front cape, right side

① Fold the drawstring over four times to give a width of 5/16 in (0.8 cm) and stitch.
② Fold the drawstring in half and attach it where the shoulder seam line meets the neckline. Stitch two or three times, one row on top of the other.

pattern D

D3

Shift ☛ page 07

★ **Pattern pieces**

D front bodice D back bodice D3 front yoke D3 back yoke D3 front neckline facing D3 back neckline facing D3 cuff facing

Cut the decorative band, bow tie, and bow knot to the measurements shown in the cutting layout for fabric B.

★ **Materials**

Fabric A (thick cotton, plain):
  W 53⅞ in x L 35⅜ in (1.37 m x 0.9 m)
Fabric B (thick cotton, striped):
  W 53⅞ in x L 27⅝ in (1.37 m x 0.7 m)

★ **For more detailed sewing instructions ▼, see pp. 53 to 55**

● Zigzag or overlock the seam allowance of the neckline facing, cuff facings, bodice hem, and slit opening. ▼

1 Sew together the bodices and yokes at both front and back. Zigzag the seam allowances on both pieces of fabric at the same time to finish them and then turn them toward the bodice.

2 Attach the decorative band to the front bodice. → Figure below.

3 Sew the shoulders. Zigzag the seam allowances on both pieces of fabric at the same time to finish them, and then turn them toward the back.

4 Edge-stitch the neckline with the facing (▼) and then blindstitch the edge of the facing.

5 Sew from the sleeve seams to the side seams. ▼

6 Finish the hem and slit. → Figure page 57.

7 Edge-stitch the cuffs with the facing (▼) and then blindstitch the edge of the facing.

8 Make and attach the bow tie. → Figure below.

Cutting layout

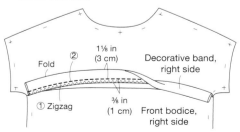

Fabric B   Back neckline facing (x 1)

27⅝ in (70 cm)

Bow tie (x 1)   Decorative band (x 1)
XS 21⅝ in (55 cm)
S 22⅞ in (58 cm)
M 24 in (61 cm)
L 25¼ in (64 cm)

3⅛ in (8 cm)   3⅛ in (8 cm)

31½ in (80 cm)

3⅛ in (8 cm)

Bow knot (x 1)
2¾ in (7 cm)

Front yoke (x 1)

Back yoke (x 1)
Cut on fold

Cuff facing (x 2)

0   0   0

Front neckline facing (x 1)

W 53⅞ in (137 cm)

Fabric A

35⅜ in (90 cm)

Cut on fold   Cut on fold

Back bodice (x 1)

Front bodice (x 1)

1⅛ in (3 cm)   1⅛ in (3 cm)

1⅛ in (3 cm)   ¹⁵⁄₁₆ in (2.5 cm)   ¹⁵⁄₁₆ in (2.5 cm)   1⅛ in (3 cm)

W 53⅞ in (137 cm)

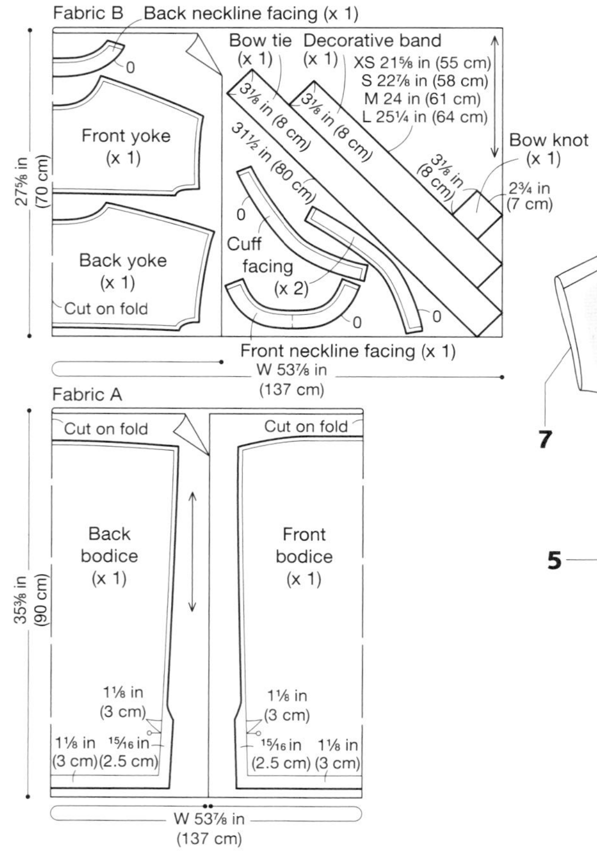

* Unless stipulated, the seam allowance is ⅜ in (1 cm)

3   4
1
2
8
7
5
6
Front
Back

2 Attach the decorative band to the front bodice

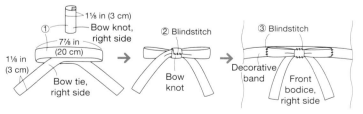

1⅛ in (3 cm)

Fold   ②

Decorative band, right side

⅜ in (1 cm)

① Zigzag   Front bodice, right side

① Fold the decorative band in half (right side out) and zigzag the raw edge.

② Stitch the decorative band in position on the front yoke.

8 Make and attach the bow tie

1⅛ in (3 cm)   Bow knot, right side

①   7⅞ in (20 cm)

1⅛ in (3 cm)   Bow tie, right side

② Blindstitch

Bow knot

③ Blindstitch

Decorative band   Front bodice, right side

① Sew the bow tie and bow knot to a width of 1⅛ in (3 cm) and turn right side out.

② Make the bow tie piece into a bow, bind the center of the bow with the bow knot, and then blindstitch.

③ Blindstitch the finished bow to the center front of the decorative band on the front bodice.

E1

Sundress → page 25

★ Pattern pieces

E front bodice **E** back bodice **E** front and back skirt
E1 pocket **E1** pocket welt fabric

★ Materials

Fabric A (linen): W 59 in x L 27⅝ in (1.5 m x 0.7 m)
Fabric B (linen):
    XS/S—W 59 in x L 114⅛ in (1.5 m x 2.9 m)
    M/L—W 59 in x L 118⅛ in (1.5 m x 3 m)
Fusible stay tape (half-bias):
    W ⅜ in x L 39⅜ in (1 cm x 1 m)
Grosgrain ribbon:
    XS/S—W 9⁄16 in x L 196⅞ in (1.5 cm x 5 m)
    M/L—W 9⁄16 in x L 216½ in (1.5 cm x 5.5 m)

★ Sewing tips

● Attach the grosgrain ribbon before you sew the bodice and skirt together.
● The bodice is lined. The front and back bodices each comprise a top and under piece.

Cutting layout

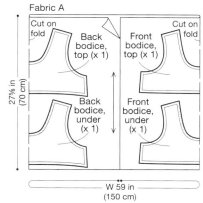

Fabric A

Cut on fold — Back bodice, top (x 1) — Front bodice, top (x 1) — Cut on fold

Back bodice, under (x 1) — Front bodice, under (x 1)

27⅝ in (70 cm)

W 59 in (150 cm)

* Unless stipulated, the seam allowance is ⅜ in (1 cm)
* ▭ Attach the fusible interfacing here

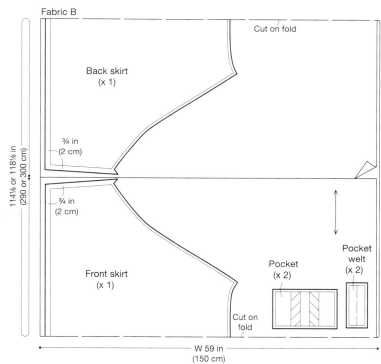

Fabric B

Cut on fold

Back skirt (x 1)

¾ in (2 cm)

¾ in (2 cm)

114⅛ or 118⅛ in (290 or 300 cm)

Front skirt (x 1)

Cut on fold

Pocket (x 2)

Pocket welt (x 2)

W 59 in (150 cm)

1 Attach the grosgrain ribbon

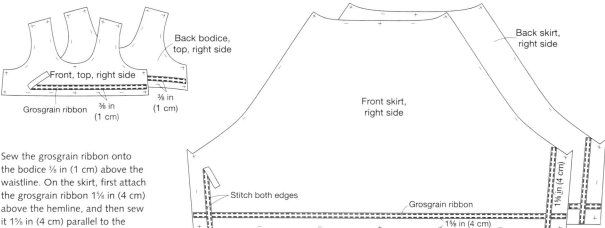

Back bodice, top, right side

Front, top, right side

Grosgrain ribbon — ⅜ in (1 cm) — ⅜ in (1 cm)

Back skirt, right side

Front skirt, right side

Stitch both edges

Grosgrain ribbon

1⅝ in (4 cm)

1⅝ in (4 cm)

1⅝ in (4 cm)

Sew the grosgrain ribbon onto the bodice ⅜ in (1 cm) above the waistline. On the skirt, first attach the grosgrain ribbon 1⅝ in (4 cm) above the hemline, and then sew it 1⅝ in (4 cm) parallel to the side seams.

2 Sew the neckline and armholes

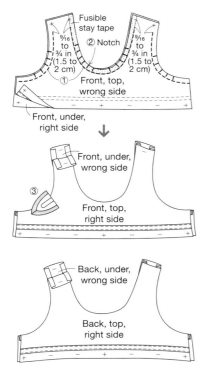

① Align the top front bodice and under front bodice wrong side out, and then sew the neckline and armholes to between ⁹⁄₁₆ and ¾ in (1.5 and 2 cm) from the shoulders.
② Add notches to the seam allowance of the curved neckline and armholes.
③ Turn right side out and iron neatly in place. Fold the seam allowance at the unsewn part of the shoulders. Sew the neckline and armholes of the back bodice in the same way.

Sewing sequence

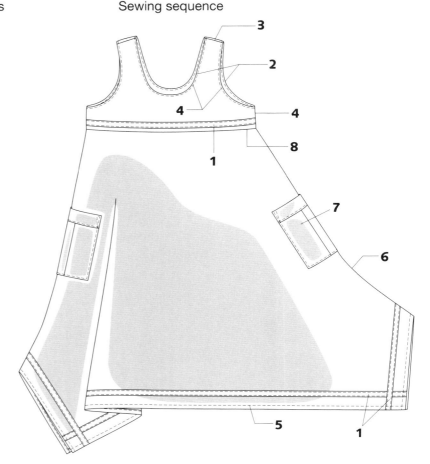

3 Sew the shoulders

① Align the shoulders of the top front bodice and top back bodice wrong side out and sew.
② Open the seam allowance and set neatly in place.
③ Fold in and then blindstitch the shoulder seam allowance of the under bodice.

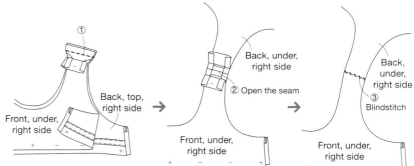

4 Sew the sides of the bodice, and then stitch the neckline and armholes

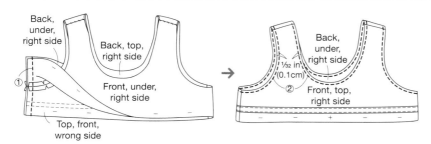

① Align the sides of the top and under bodices wrong side out and then sew them as one seam. Open the seam allowance.
② Iron the armholes neatly in place and then stitch the armholes and the neckline.

5 Finish the hem

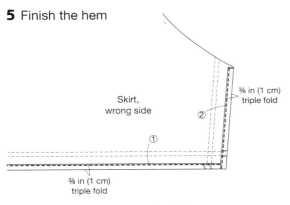

Skirt, wrong side

③⁄₈ in (1 cm) triple fold

②

①

③⁄₈ in (1 cm) triple fold

① Stitch the hem of the front and back skirt pieces with a threefold hem.
② Stitch the sides with a threefold hem.

7 Attach the pockets

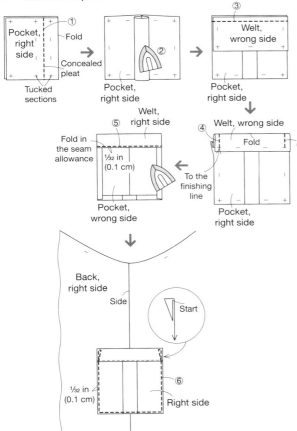

Pocket, right side
①
Fold
Concealed pleat
Tucked sections

Pocket, right side
②

③
Welt, wrong side
Pocket, right side

④
Welt, wrong side
Fold
④
Pocket, right side

⑤
Welt, right side
Fold in the seam allowance
¹⁄₃₂ in (0.1 cm)
To the finishing line
Pocket, wrong side

Back, right side
Side
Start
¹⁄₃₂ in (0.1 cm)
⑥
Right side

① Fold the pockets right side out and sew the concealed pleats.
② Fold the tucks and iron neatly in place.
③ Align the pocket welts and pockets wrong side out and sew together.
④ Fold the welts wrong side out and sew both sides.
⑤ Turn the welts right side out. Fold the seam allowance around the pocket, fold in the seam allowance on the wrong side of the welts and iron neatly in place, and then topstitch the bottom edge of the welts.
⑥ Sew the pockets in position on the skirt. The corners of the welts must be able to withstand force, so stitch them with a triangle shape.

6 Sew the sides of the skirt

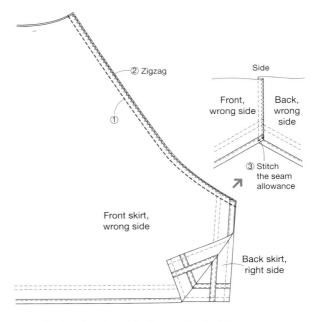

② Zigzag

①

Side
Front, wrong side
Back, wrong side

③ Stitch the seam allowance

Front skirt, wrong side

Back skirt, right side

① Align the sides of the front and back skirt wrong side out and sew.
② Zigzag the seam allowance on both layers together to finish.
③ Turn the seam allowance toward the back, iron neatly in place, and then stitch to secure the hem section.

8 Sew the bodice and skirt together

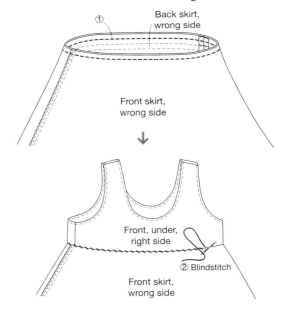

①
Back skirt, wrong side

Front skirt, wrong side

Front, under, right side

② Blindstitch

Front skirt, wrong side

① Align the waists of the top bodice and skirt wrong side out and sew, lifting the under bodice out of the way.
② Turn the seam allowance toward the bodice and iron neatly in place, then fold the seam allowance of the under bodice inside and blindstitch.

pattern E

E2

Sundress → page 24

★ **Pattern pieces**

E front bodice E back bodice E front and back skirt
E2 front and back drawstring tunnel band

★ **Materials**

Fabric A (cotton broadcloth):
  W 43¼ in x L 27⅝ in (1.1 m x 0.7 m)
Fabric B (printed cotton lawn):
  XS/S: W 43¼ in x L 114⅛ in (1.1 m x 2.9 m)
  M/L: W 43¼ in x L 118⅛ in (1.1 m x 3 m)
Fusible interfacing: W 35⅜ in x L 27⅝ in (90 cm x 70 cm)
Satin ribbon: W ¼ in x L 118⅛ in (0.6 cm x 3 m)

★ **For more detailed sewing instructions ▼,
see pp. 60 and 61**

● Attach the fusible interfacing to the wrong side of the under bodice. Zigzag or overlock the side seam allowances of the skirt.
1 Sew the neckline and armholes. ▼
2 Sew the shoulders. ▼
3 Sew the sides of the bodice, and then stitch the neckline and armholes. ▼
4 Stitch the hem with a threefold hem. ▼
5 Sew the sides of the skirt, ensuring that you leave an opening on each side for the drawstring tunnel, and open the seam allowance.
6 Attach the drawstring tunnel band. → Figure below.
7 Sew the bodice and skirt together. ▼
8 Pass a 59 in (1.5 m) length of satin ribbon through the front and back drawstring tunnels. Stitch the ends of the satin ribbon with a threefold hem.

Cutting layout

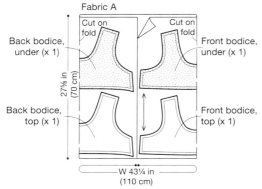

Fabric A

Cut on fold

Back bodice, under (x 1)

Cut on fold

Front bodice, under (x 1)

27⅝ in (70 cm)

Back bodice, top (x 1)

Front bodice, top (x 1)

W 43¼ in (110 cm)

* Unless stipulated, the seam allowance is ⅜ in (1 cm)
* ▒ Attach the fusible interfacing here

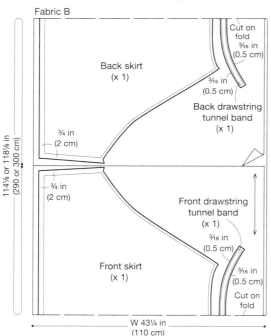

Fabric B

Back skirt (x 1)

Cut on fold
3/16 in (0.5 cm)

3/16 in (0.5 cm)

Back drawstring tunnel band (x 1)

114⅛ in or 118⅛ in (290 or 300 cm)

¾ in (2 cm)

¾ in (2 cm)

Front drawstring tunnel band (x 1)

3/16 in (0.5 cm)

Front skirt (x 1)

3/16 in (0.5 cm)

Cut on fold

W 43¼ in (110 cm)

Sewing sequence

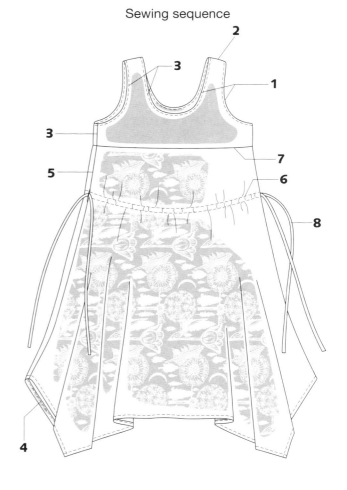

2
3
1
3
7
5
6
8
4

6 Attach the drawstring tunnel band

① Sew the ends of the front and back drawstring tunnel bands to form a loop.
② Fold the seam allowance of the drawstring tunnel band with an iron.
③ Align the drawstring tunnel band at the position where it will be attached to the wrong side of the skirt and stitch in place.

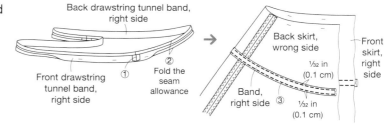

Back drawstring tunnel band, right side

Front drawstring tunnel band, right side

① ② Fold the seam allowance

Back skirt, wrong side

Front skirt, right side

1/32 in (0.1 cm)

Band, right side ③

1/32 in (0.1 cm)

pattern E

E3

Dress/skirt
➜ page 26

★ **Pattern pieces**
E front and back skirt
Cut the bodice to the measurements shown in the cutting layout for fabric A.

★ **Materials**
Fabric A (rib-knit):
XS/S—Tubular knit W 13 in x L 27⅝ in (33 cm x 70 cm)
M/L—Tubular knit W 13 in x L 55⅛ in (33 cm x 1.4 m)
Fabric B (linen):
XS/S—W 59 in x L 114⅛ in (1.5 m x 2.9 m)
M/L—W 59 in x L 118⅛ in (1.5 m x 3 m)

★ **Sewing tips**
● Fabric A is a tubular rib-knit. For sizes XS and S, use the tubular knit just as it comes to make the bodices, cutting a single piece. If you cannot find tubular rib-knit and are using a flat rib-knit, fit the fabric to yourself using the pattern measurements as a guide.
● See page 59 for the cutting layout for fabric B.

★ **For more detailed sewing instructions ▼, see p. 61**
1 Stitch the hem with a threefold hem. ▼
2 Sew the sides of the skirt. ▼
3 Sew the waists together → Figure below. For sizes M and L, stitch the sides of the front and back bodices before sewing the waists together.

Cutting layout

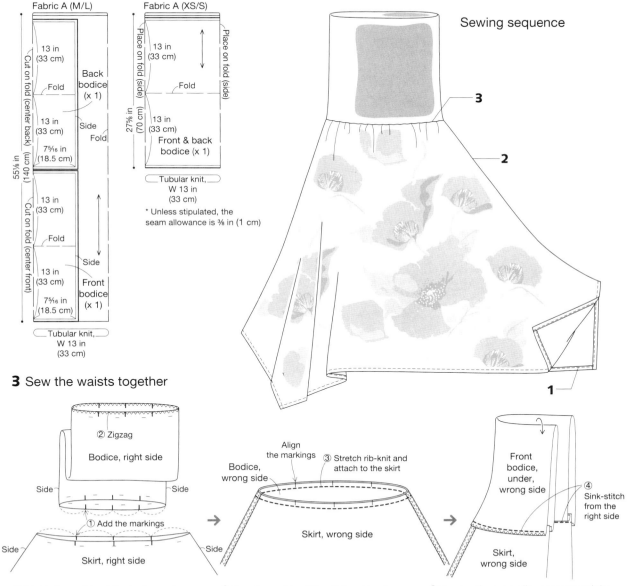

3 Sew the waists together

① Divide the waists of the bodice and skirt into four equal sections, marking them off.
② Finish one face of the bodice by zigzagging or overlocking. This face will form the under bodice.

③ Turn the waists of the skirt and bodice wrong side out, align the markings, and sew, stretching the rib-knit of the bodice as you do so.

④ Turning the seam allowance toward the bodice, fold the bodice over, and right side out, to align the markings, and sink-stitch the waist from the right side to attach the under bodice. Make sure that you stretch the bodice as you sew.

pattern F

F1

Sundress ➔ page 28

★ Pattern pieces

F front bodice **F1** bust design panel

Widen the front bodice by 3⅞ in (10 cm) at the center front and 2 in (5 cm) at the sides, as shown in the full-scale pattern piece, and extend the measurement shown in the full-scale pattern layout **F3** from the hem. Make rectangular pattern pieces for the back bodice, shoulder straps, and back facing using the measurements shown in the cutting layout.

★ Materials

Fabric (cotton):

XS/S—W 47¼ in x L 82⅝ in (1.2 m x 2.1 m)

M/L—W 47¼ in x L 86⅝ in (1.2 m x 2.2 m)

Facing (lightweight cotton):

W 43¼ in x L 3⅞ in (1.1 m x 0.1 m)

Fusible interfacing: W 11¾ in x L 27⅝ in (30 x 70 cm)

Elastic (soft): W 1⅛ in (3 cm), length to suit

★ Sewing tip

- Attach the fusible interfacing to the wrong side of the bust design panel.

Cutting layout

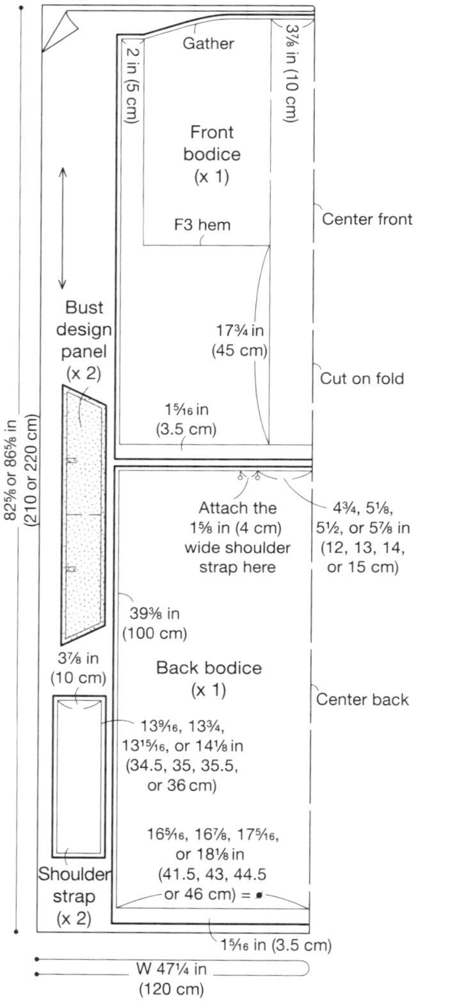

Fabric
Gather
2 in (5 cm)
3⅞ in (10 cm)
Front bodice (x 1)
F3 hem
Center front
Bust design panel (x 2)
17¾ in (45 cm)
Cut on fold
1 5/16 in (3.5 cm)
82⅝ or 86⅝ in (210 or 220 cm)
Attach the 1⅝ in (4 cm) wide shoulder strap here
4¾, 5⅛, 5½, or 5⅞ in (12, 13, 14, or 15 cm)
39⅜ in (100 cm)
3⅞ in (10 cm)
Back bodice (x 1)
Center back
13 9/16, 13¾, 13 15/16, or 14⅛ in (34.5, 35, 35.5, or 36 cm)
16 5/16, 16⅞, 17 5/16, or 18⅛ in (41.5, 43, 44.5 or 46 cm) = •
Shoulder strap (x 2)
1 5/16 in (3.5 cm)
W 47¼ in (120 cm)

* Unless stipulated, the seam allowance is ⅜ in (1 cm)

* [shaded box] Attach the fusible interfacing here

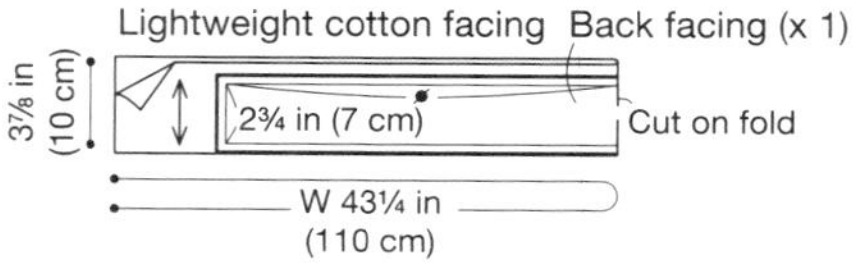

Lightweight cotton facing
Back facing (x 1)
3⅞ in (10 cm)
2¾ in (7 cm)
Cut on fold
W 43¼ in (110 cm)

Sewing sequence

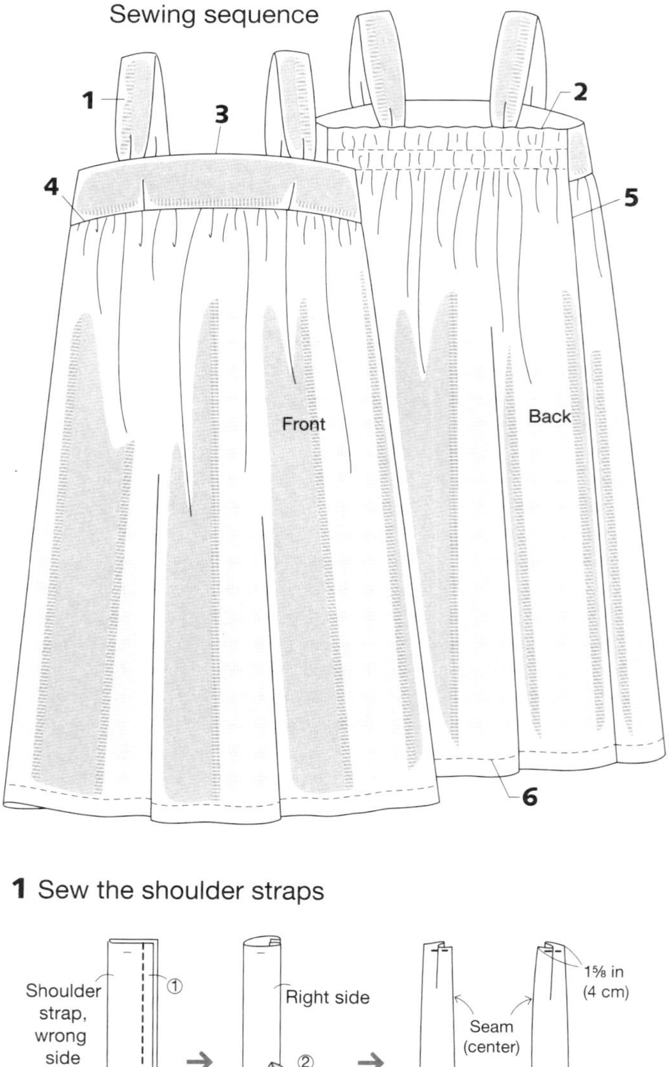

1
2
3
4
5
6
Front
Back

1 Sew the shoulder straps

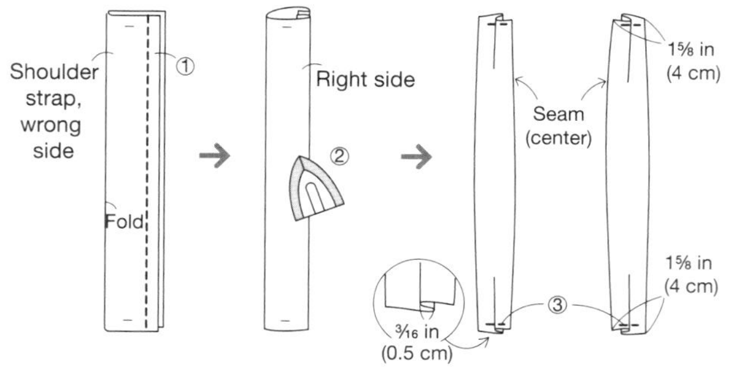

Shoulder strap, wrong side
①
Fold
Right side
②
Seam (center)
1⅝ in (4 cm)
1⅝ in (4 cm)
③
3/16 in (0.5 cm)

① Fold the shoulder straps wrong side out and stitch.

② Turn right side out and iron neatly.

③ Fold a tuck in both ends of the two layers of fabric at the same time, and then baste or stitch in place. Repeat to make the second shoulder strap.

2 Attach the facing, sandwiching the shoulder straps, and pass the elastic through

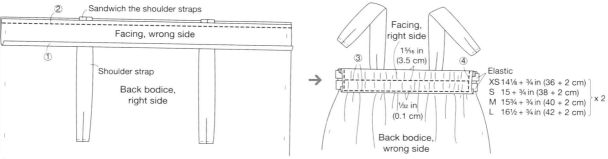

② Sandwich the shoulder straps
Facing, wrong side
① Shoulder strap
Back bodice, right side

Facing, right side
③ 1⁵⁄₁₆ in (3.5 cm) ④
1⁄₃₂ in (0.1 cm)
Back bodice, wrong side

Elastic
XS 14⅛ + ¾ in (36 + 2 cm)
S 15 + ¾ in (38 + 2 cm)   } × 2
M 15¾ + ¾ in (40 + 2 cm)
L 16½ + ¾ in (42 + 2 cm)

① Fold the seam allowance of the bottom edge of the facing.
② Align the back bodice and facing wrong side out and stitch, sandwiching the shoulder straps.

③ Turn the facing right side out, iron neatly in place, and stitch in two rows.
④ Pass the elastic between the stitches, and then attach the ends to the seam allowance of the sides.

3 Sew the bust design panel, sandwiching the shoulder straps

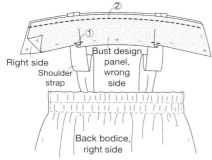

②
①
Right side
Shoulder strap
Bust design panel, wrong side
Back bodice, right side

① Fold the tucks in the bust design panel and baste or stitch in place.
② Align the two layers of the bust design panel wrong side out and stitch, sandwiching the shoulder straps. Turn right side out and iron neatly in place.

4 Attach the bust design panel to the front bodice

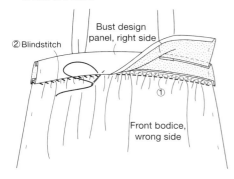

② Blindstitch
Bust design panel, right side
①
Front bodice, wrong side

① Sew a row of large stitches in the seam allowance at the top edge of the front bodice, add the gathers, and then align wrong side out with the bust design panel (right side out), and stitch together.
② Fold the seam allowance at the bottom of the bust design panel (wrong side out) and then blindstitch along the seam in ①.

5 Sew the sides

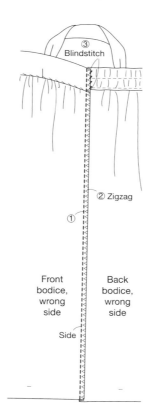

③ Blindstitch
② Zigzag
①
Front bodice, wrong side
Back bodice, wrong side
Side

① Align the front and back sides wrong side out and sew.
② Finish both seam allowances at the same time by zigzagging or overlocking.
③ Turn the seam allowance toward the back, blindstitching only the back facing section.

6 Finish the hem

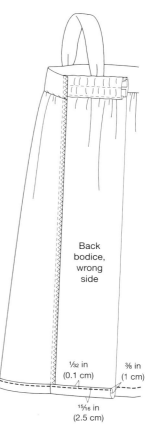

Back bodice, wrong side
1⁄₃₂ in (0.1 cm)
⅜ in (1 cm)
1⁵⁄₁₆ in (2.5 cm)

Stitch the seam allowance of the hem with a 1⁵⁄₁₆ in (2.5 cm) wide threefold hem.

F2

Shift → page 29

★ Pattern pieces

F front bodice **F2** bust design panel
On the front bodice, extend the measurement shown in full-scale pattern layout **F3** from the hem. Make rectangular pattern pieces for the back bodice, back facing, shoulder straps, and ruffles A and B using the measurements shown in the cutting layout.

★ Materials

Fabric (printed cotton lawn):
   XS/S—W 43¼ in x L 106¼ in (1.1 m x 2.7 m)
   M/L—W 43¼ in x L 110¼ in (1.1 m x 2.8 m)
Fusible interfacing: W 11¾ in x L 27⅝ in (30 x 70 cm)
Elastic (soft): W 1⅛ in (3 cm), length to suit

★ For more detailed sewing instructions ▼, see pp. 64 and 65

- Attach the fusible interfacing to the wrong side of the bust design panel. Zigzag or overlock the hem and the top and bottom of ruffles A and B.
1. Sew the shoulder straps. ▼
2. Sandwich the shoulder straps between the back bodice and the facing. Attach the facing and pass the elastic through. ▼
3. Sew the bust design panel, sandwiching the shoulder straps. ▼
4. Gather the front bodice and attach the bust design panel. ▼
5. Make the ruffles A and B and attach them to the front bodice. → Figure below.
6. Sew the sides as far as the slit ends. ▼
7. Fold up and blindstitch the hem, and then stitch the seam allowance of the slits with a threefold hem.

Cutting layout

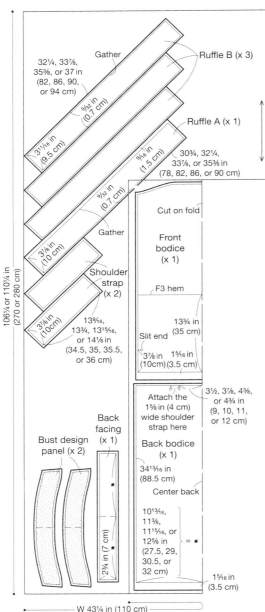

Gather
Ruffle B (x 3)
32¼, 33⅞, 35⅜, or 37 in (82, 86, 90, or 94 cm)
9/32 in (0.7 cm)
Ruffle A (x 1)
3 1/16 in (9.5 cm)
9/16 in (1.5 cm)
30¾, 32¼, 33⅞, or 35⅜ in (78, 82, 86, or 90 cm)
9/32 in (0.7 cm)
Gather
3⅞ in (10 cm)
Shoulder strap (x 2)
3⅞ in (10cm)
13 9/16, 13¾, 13 15/16, or 14⅛ in (34.5, 35, 35.5, or 36 cm)

Cut on fold
Front bodice (x 1)
F3 hem
13¾ in (35 cm)
Slit end
3⅞ in (10cm)   1 5/16 in (3.5 cm)

106¼ or 110¼ in (270 or 280 cm)

Bust design panel (x 2)
Back facing (x 1)
2¾ in (7 cm)

Attach the 1⅝ in (4 cm) wide shoulder strap here
3½, 3⅞, 4⅜, or 4¾ in (9, 10, 11, or 12 cm)
Back bodice (x 1)
34 13/16 in (88.5 cm)
Center back
10 13/16, 11⅜, 11 15/16, or 12⅝ in (27.5, 29, 30.5, or 32 cm)
= ●
1 5/16 in (3.5 cm)

W 43¼ in (110 cm)

* Unless stipulated, the seam allowance is ⅜ in (1 cm)
* ░░ Attach the fusible interfacing here
* Where four measurements are given, they represent the sizes XS/S/M/L in that order

Sewing sequence

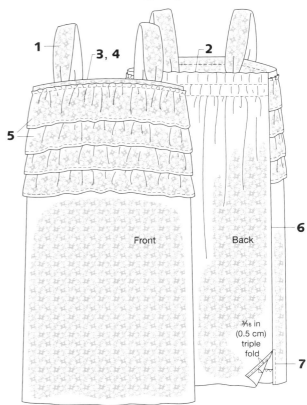

1
3, 4
2
5
Front
Back
6
3/16 in (0.5 cm) triple fold
7

5 Make the ruffles A and B and attach them to the front bodice

Fold and stitch the seam allowance at the bottom of the ruffles, and then gather the top edges. When attaching the ruffles, stitch over the top of the gather stitches, working in sequence from the lowest ruffle up. For ruffle A, see page 67. Attach the sides of the ruffles to the side seam allowances of the bodice.

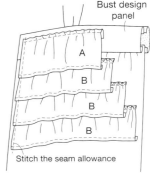

Bust design panel
A
B
B
B
Stitch the seam allowance

pattern F

F3

Tunic ✿ *page 19*

★ Pattern pieces

F front bodice **F3** bust design panel

Make pattern pieces for the back bodice, back facing, shoulder straps, ruffle, and ribbon using the measurements shown in the cutting layout.

★ Materials

Fabric (cotton and linen, double sided):
　　XS/S—W 43¼ in x L 74¾ in (1.1 m x 1.9 m)
　　M/L—W 43¼ in x L 78¾ in (1.1 m x 2 m)
Lightweight fusible interfacing:
　　W 35⅜ in x L 11¾ in (90 cm x 30 cm)
Elastic (soft): W 1⅛ in (3 cm), length to suit

★ Sewing tip

● The fabric is double faced, with polka dots and stripes. Sew the bust design panel, shoulder straps, and ruffle with the striped side up, the ribbon with both stripe and polka dot, and other components with the polka dot side.

★ For more detailed sewing instructions ▼, see pp. 64 and 65

● Attach the fusible interfacing to the wrong side of the bust design panel. Zigzag or overlock the hem and the top and bottom of the ruffle.
1. Sew the shoulder straps. ▼
2. Sandwich the shoulder straps between the back bodice and the facing. Attach the facing and pass the elastic through. ▼
3. Sew the bust design panel, sandwiching the shoulder straps. ▼
4. Gather the front bodice and attach the bust design panel. ▼
5. Make the ruffle and attach it to the front bodice. → Figure below.
6. Sew the sides. ▼
7. Fold up the hem and blindstitch.
8. Make the ribbon. Align the two faces (polka dot and stripe) and edge-stitch, leaving an opening for turning out. Turn right side out and blindstitch the opening.

Cutting layout

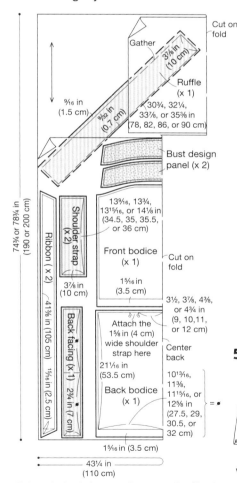

* Unless stipulated, the seam allowance is ⅜ in (1 cm)
* ░░░ Attach the fusible interfacing here
* ▦ Use the striped side as the right side
* Where four measurements are given, they represent the sizes XS/S/M/L in that order

Sewing sequence

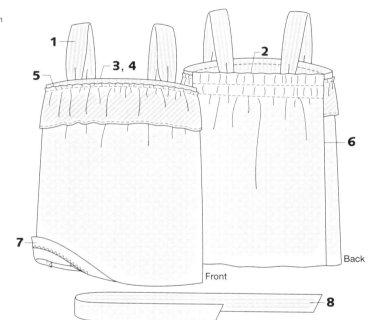

5 Make the ruffle and attach it to the front bodice

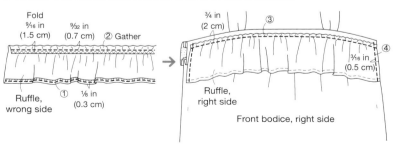

① Fold and stitch the seam allowance at the bottom of the ruffle.
② Fold the seam allowance at the top of the ruffle, sew with large stitches, and then gather.

③ Attach the ruffle to the bust design panel, stitching over the top of the gather stitches.
④ Attach the sides of the ruffle to the side seam allowances of the bodice.

pattern G

G1

Sundress ➜ page 30

★ Pattern piece

G1 bra top
Make the pattern pieces for the front bodice, back bodice, and sash using the measurements in your cutting draft. Cut the bias binding to the measurements shown in the cutting layout.

★ Materials

Fabric (cotton):
   XS/S—W 42½ in x L 118⅛ in (1.08 m x 3 m)
   M/L—W 42½ in x L 125⅞ in (1.08 m x 3.2 m)
Grosgrain ribbon: W ⅜ in x L 118⅛ in (1 cm x 3 m)
Elastic (soft): W 1⅛ in (3 cm), length to suit
Buttons: ½ in (1.3 cm) diameter x 2

★ Sewing tip

● Once you have passed the grosgrain ribbon through the bra top, use the buttons on the inside of the back bodice to hold it in place. Alternatively, you could put the buttons on the outside of the bodice.

Cutting draft

Sewing sequence

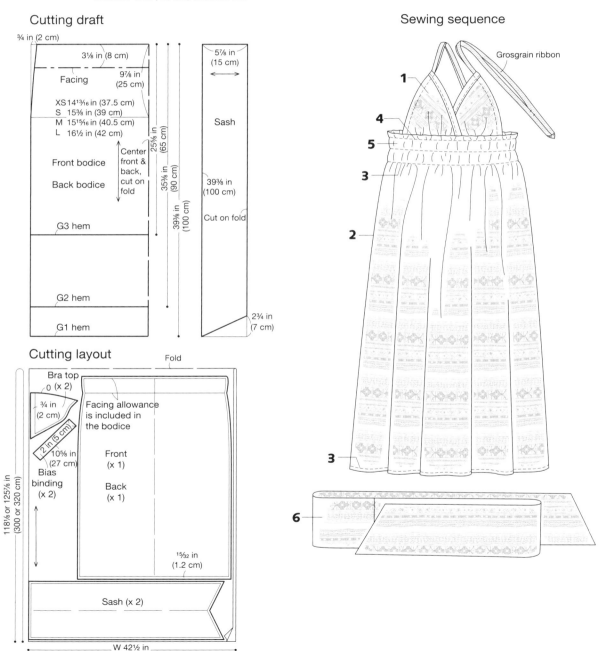

¾ in (2 cm)

3⅛ in (8 cm)

5⅞ in (15 cm)

Facing

9⅞ in (25 cm)

XS 14¹³⁄₁₆ in (37.5 cm)
S 15⅜ in (39 cm)
M 15¹⁵⁄₁₆ in (40.5 cm)
L 16½ in (42 cm)

Sash

25⅝ in (65 cm)

Center front & back, cut on fold

Front bodice

Back bodice

35⅜ in (90 cm)

39⅜ in (100 cm)

39⅜ in (100 cm)

Cut on fold

G3 hem

G2 hem

G1 hem

2¾ in (7 cm)

Grosgrain ribbon

Cutting layout

Fold

Bra top
0 (x 2)

¾ in (2 cm)

2 in (5 cm)

10⅝ in (27 cm)

Bias binding (x 2)

Facing allowance is included in the bodice

Front (x 1)

Back (x 1)

1⁵⁄₃₂ in (1.2 cm)

118⅛ or 125⅞ in (300 or 320 cm)

Sash (x 2)

W 42½ in (108 cm)

* Unless stipulated, the seam allowance is ⅜ in (1 cm)

1 Make the bra tops

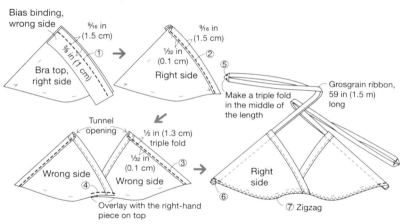

Bias binding, wrong side

⁹⁄₁₆ in (1.5 cm)

³⁄₈ in (1 cm) ①

Bra top, right side

⁹⁄₁₆ in (1.5 cm)

①

1/32 in (0.1 cm) ②

Right side

⑤

Make a triple fold in the middle of the length

Grosgrain ribbon, 59 in (1.5 m) long

Tunnel opening

½ in (1.3 cm) triple fold

Wrong side ④

1/32 in (0.1 cm) ③

Wrong side

Overlay with the right-hand piece on top

Right side

⑥

⑦ Zigzag

① Align the bias binding wrong side out with the top point of the bra top and stitch ⁹⁄₁₆ in (1.5 cm) from the edge that has no seam allowance.

② Bind with the bias binding and stitch. Repeat.

③ Stitch the side seam allowances with a ½ in (1.3 cm) wide threefold hem to create a tunnel.

④ Lay the center fronts of the two bra tops over one another with the right-hand piece on top and then stitch the seam allowance in place.

⑤ Fold each 59 in (1.5 m) length of grosgrain ribbon into a triangle at the middle, and then stitch.

⑥ Pass each length of grosgrain ribbon through the tunnels in the sides of the bra tops, and stitch the ends to hold them in place.

⑦ Zigzag or overlock the seam allowance of the bottom edges.

2 Sew the sides

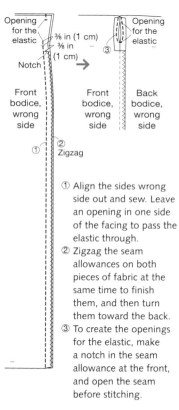

Opening for the elastic

³⁄₈ in (1 cm)
³⁄₈ in (1 cm)

Notch

③

Opening for the elastic

Front bodice, wrong side

Front bodice, wrong side

Back bodice, wrong side

① ② Zigzag

① Align the sides wrong side out and sew. Leave an opening in one side of the facing to pass the elastic through.

② Zigzag the seam allowances on both pieces of fabric at the same time to finish them, and then turn them toward the back.

③ To create the openings for the elastic, make a notch in the seam allowance at the front, and open the seam before stitching.

3 Finish the top edge and hem

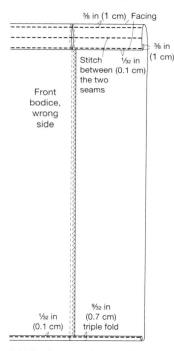

³⁄₈ in (1 cm) Facing

Stitch between the two seams

1/32 in (0.1 cm)

³⁄₈ in (1 cm)

Front bodice, wrong side

1/32 in (0.1 cm)

9/32 in (0.7 cm) triple fold

Fold the facing at the top edge and stitch in three rows. Stitch the hem with a threefold hem.

4 Attach the bra tops

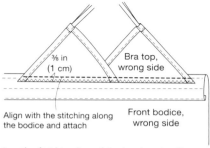

³⁄₈ in (1 cm)

Bra top, wrong side

Align with the stitching along the bodice and attach

Front bodice, wrong side

Lay the finishing line of the bra tops to align with the stitching along the top edge of the front bodice, wrong side, and then stitch.

5 Pass the elastic through the facing and attach the buttons

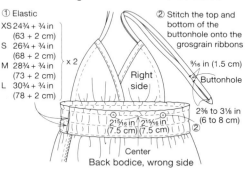

① Elastic

XS 24¾ + ¾ in (63 + 2 cm)
S 26¾ + ¾ in (68 + 2 cm)
M 28¾ + ¾ in (73 + 2 cm)
L 30¾ + ¾ in (78 + 2 cm)

x 2

② Stitch the top and bottom of the buttonhole onto the grosgrain ribbons

⁹⁄₁₆ in (1.5 cm)

Buttonhole

Right side

2³⁄₈ to 3⅛ in (6 to 8 cm)

2¹⁵⁄₁₆ in (7.5 cm) 2¹⁵⁄₁₆ in (7.5 cm)

②

Center
Back bodice, wrong side

① Pass the elastic through the two tunnels in the facing, and stitch the ends with an overlap of around ¾ in (2 cm). Blindstitch the openings, then topstitch from the right side of the fabric onto the left and right side seams to hold the elastic in place. To determine the length of the elastic and the position of the buttonholes, do a trial fitting with the measurements in the drawings as your guideline.

② Attach the buttons to the facing, and make the buttonholes by stitching the grosgrain ribbons as shown.

6 Make the sash

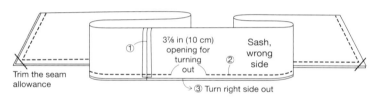

Trim the seam allowance

①

3⅞ in (10 cm) opening for turning out

②

Sash, wrong side

③ Turn right side out

① Sew the two pieces together to create a single length.

② Fold wrong side out and sew, leaving an opening for turning out.

③ Pull the sash through the opening to turn the fabric right side out, iron neatly, and blindstitch the opening.

pattern G
G2
Skirt/dress
❦ page 16

★ **Pattern pieces**
Make the pattern pieces for the front bodice, back bodice, facing, and sash using the measurements in the cutting draft on page 68.

★ **Materials**
Fabric (polka dot embroidered linen):
    W 45¼ in x L 102⅜ in (1.15 m x 2.6 m)
Facing (lightweight cotton):
    W 35⅜ in x L 7⅞ in (90 cm x 20 cm)
Elastic (soft): W 1⅛ in (3 cm), length to suit

★ **For more detailed sewing instructions ▼, see p. 69**

1 Sew the sides. Finish both seam allowances at the same time by zigzagging or overlocking and turn to one side.
2 Finish the hem by zigzagging, and then fold onto the finishing line and stitch.
3 Edge-stitch the top edge with the facing.
    → Figure below.
4 Pass the elastic through the facing. ▼
5 Make the sash. ▼

Cutting layout

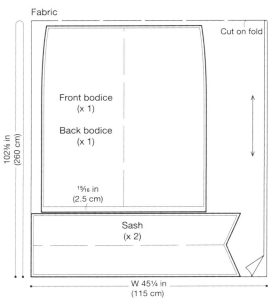

Fabric

102⅜ in (260 cm)

Cut on fold

Front bodice (x 1)

Back bodice (x 1)

1⁵⁄₁₆ in (2.5 cm)

Sash (x 2)

W 45¼ in (115 cm)

* Unless stipulated, the seam allowance is ⅜ in (1 cm)

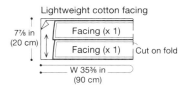

Lightweight cotton facing

7⅞ in (20 cm)

Facing (x 1)
Facing (x 1)   Cut on fold

W 35⅜ in (90 cm)

Sewing sequence

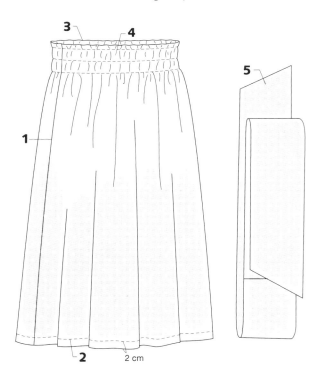

3
4
5
1
2   2 cm

3 Edge-stitch the top edge with the facing

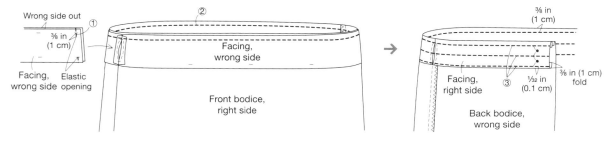

Wrong side out
①
⅜ in (1 cm)
②
Facing, wrong side
Front bodice, right side
Facing, wrong side   Elastic opening

⅜ in (1 cm)
Facing, right side   ③   ¹⁄₃₂ in (0.1 cm)   ⅜ in (1 cm) fold
Back bodice, wrong side

① Sew the sides of the facing. On one side, leave an opening for the elastic, opening and stitching the seam allowance.

② Align the bodice and facing wrong side out and sew.

③ Turn the facing right side out, set neatly in place, and stitch in place in three rows.

pattern G

G3

Tunic ☞ page 08

★ Pattern pieces

Make the pattern pieces for the front bodice, back bodice, and facing using the measurements in the cutting draft on page 68. Cut the shoulder straps to the measurements shown in the cutting layout.

★ Materials

Fabric (linen): W 59 in x L 59 in (1.5 m x 1.5 m)
Facing (lightweight cotton):
   W 35⅜ in x L 7⅞ in (90 cm x 20 cm)
Elastic (soft): W 1⅛ in (3 cm), length to suit

★ Sewing instructions

1 Sew the sides. Finish both seam allowances at the same time by zigzagging or overlocking and turn to one side.
2 Finish the hem by zigzagging, and then fold onto the finishing line and stitch.
3 Make the shoulder straps. Fold the four shoulder strap pieces over four times to a width of ¹⁵/₃₂ in (1.2 cm) and stitch.
4 Edge-stitch the top edge with the facing, sandwiching the shoulder straps. → Figure below.
5 Pass the elastic through the facing. For the length of the elastic, see page 69.

Cutting layout

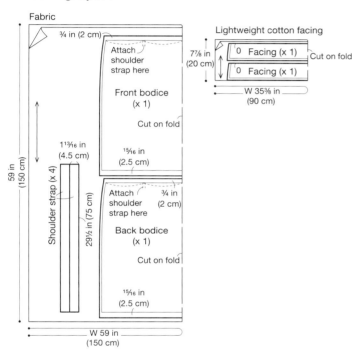

* Unless stipulated, the seam allowance is ⅜ in (1 cm)

Sewing sequence

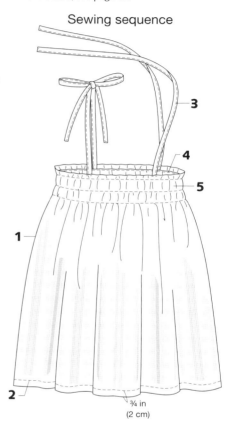

4 Edge-stitch the top edge with the facing, sandwiching the shoulder straps

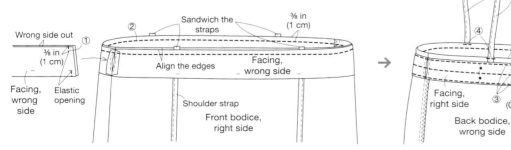

① Sew the sides of the facing. On one side, leave an opening for the elastic, opening and stitching the seam allowance.

② Turn the bodice and facing wrong side out and align the edges, then sew with a ⅜ in (1 cm) seam allowance, sandwiching the shoulder straps.

③ Turn the facing right side out, slipping it in by ⅜ in (1 cm) so that it does not show. Iron neatly, and then stitch in three rows.

④ Topstitch the shoulder straps onto the top edge of the bodice.

LAURENCE KING

Published in 2013 by
Laurence King Publishing Ltd
361–373 City Road
London EC1V 1LR
United Kingdom
Tel: + 44 20 7841 6900
Fax: + 44 20 7841 6910
e-mail: enquiries@laurenceking.com
www.laurenceking.com

FEMININE WARDROBE *OUYOUJIZAI NA PATTERN DE TSUKURU*
by Jinko Matsumoto
© Jinko Matsumoto 2010
All rights reserved
Original Japanese edition published by EDUCATIONAL FOUNDATION
BUNKA GAKUEN, BUNKA PUBLISHING BUREAU.

This English edition is published by arrangement with EDUCATIONAL
FOUNDATION BUNKA GAKUEN, BUNKA PUBLISHING BUREAU, Tokyo, in
care of Tuttle-Mori Agency, Inc., Tokyo.

Jinko Matsumoto has asserted her right under the Copyright, Designs, and
Patent Act 1988, to be identified as the Author of this Work.

A catalogue record for this book is available from the British Library.

ISBN: 978-1-78067-124-6

Printed in China

English edition
Translated from the Japanese ➤ Andy Walker
Techncial consultants ➤ Kevin Almond, Bo Breda, Chika Ito
Design ➤ Mark Holt

Japanese edition
Book design ➤ Miho Sakato
Photography ➤ Wakana Tanabe
Styling ➤ Tomoe Ito
Hair & makeup ➤ Yumi Narai
Model ➤ Iruka
Technical editor ➤ Naoko Domeki
Digital tracing ➤ Rumu Shikano
Pattern grading ➤ Kazuhiro Ueno
Operations ➤ Satomi Tokunaga
Assistance with sewing the garments ➤ Kazuko Shicchi,
  Aiko Matsumoto
Editor ➤ Yukiko Miyazaki (Bunka Publishing Bureau)
Publisher ➤ Sunao Onuma